KEATS AND MEDICINE

By the same author:

The English Channel
A Celebration of the Channel's Role in England's History

KEATS and MEDICINE

by
Hillas Smith
FRCP

PUBLISHED BY CROSS PUBLISHING
NEWPORT, ISLE OF WIGHT

First published in 1995
© Hillas Smith 1995

British Library Cataloguing in Publication Data
A catalogue record for this book is available from the British Library

ISBN 1 873295 11 1

All rights reserved. No part of this publication may be reproduced, stored in a retrieval system, or transmitted, in any form or by any means, electronic, mechanical, photocopying, recording or otherwise, without prior permission of the publisher and the author

Produced and published by Cross Publishing, Newport, Isle of Wight
Printed in Great Britain by The Bath Press, Bath, Avon

Acknowledgements

All the black and white pictures in this book are from the collections at Keats House Hampstead and are reproduced by kind permission of the London Borough of Camden.

The picture of Fanny Brawne (page 79) is taken from the miniature on display in Keats House and I am most grateful to Mr Robert Goodsell for permission to reproduce it.

The colour photograph on the dust jacket is published by kind permission of the Wellcome Institute Library London.

Contents

I	Introduction	13
II	Early Life	29
III	Why Medicine	
	(i) The Decision	37
	(ii) Apprenticeship	42
	(iii) Medical School	47
IV	Medicine and Literature	59
V	Keats and Tuberculosis	73
VI	Keats and Sexuality	85
VII	Finale	97
	Appendix I	
	Keats's Doctors	117
	Appendix II	
	Biographies of Keats	122
	Publications with Particular	
	Medical Relevance	123
	Selected Bibliography	124

List of Illustrations

Thomas Hammond's House Edmonton	43
Guy's Hospital	48
Keats in operating theatre	53
Astley Cooper	54
Charcoal drawing of Keats	55
Thomas Wakeley	56
Fanny Brawne	79
Keats House	96
Joseph Severn	107
Spanish Steps	109
Sir James Clark	110
Keats on his deathbed	112

Preface

The object of this short book is to emphasise the medical aspects of Keats's life and works to the lay or 'literary' reader, - the last attempt along these lines was by Hale-White more than half a century ago - and to introduce some of the works to medical men. The bicentenary of Keats's death gives an opportunity for reassessment of medical influences. I also hope that the book might be an introduction to Keats for the general reader. Keeping these objects in mind, and at the same time trying to placate the academics of English Literature could in fact be a prescription for disaster. I am only too well aware that in trying to please everyone I may end up pleasing nobody.

In the writing of this book I have been lucky in having the advice and support of colleagues and friends. A number of librarians have been most helpful and co-operative. Foremost among these is Mrs Christina Gee of Keats House, Hampstead from whom I have benefited not only from her knowledge and expertise in all aspects of Keats literature, but also by her constant advice and skill in many subjects allied to librarianship. I am deeply grateful for her interest and help. Maggie Van Reenen and Roberta Davis, assistant librarians at Keats House have also been most helpful and supportive. I have also had assistance from the staff of a number of other libraries: these include The British Library (Dept. of Manuscripts), Fitzwilliam Museum Cambridge, The Guildhall Library, The Wellcome Library, the libraries of the Royal College of Physicians of London and Edinburgh. To Mr T.H.E. Orde, archivist of Guy's Hospital and to Miss Fear, librarian, Royal Free Hospital I am also grateful. Janet Horncy, the Alexander Turnbull Library, Wellington, and Miss Marian Morgan of Timaru Public Library, New Zealand, have assisted in trying to trace the descendants of Dr Samuel Hammond who settled in Timaru. Juanita Burnby of Enfield has been most helpful in details relating to the Hammond family and has kindly provided me with her invaluable *The Hammonds of Edmonton*. I am most grateful to Miss Joan Sinar, Derbyshire County archivist and her staff for allowing me access to and for assistance with the voluminous correspondence of John Taylor.

I owe a special debt to Prof. Ernest Pereira of the Dept. of English, University of S.A. Pretoria, who read the original manuscript and made many constructive criticisms. I am grateful for the time and effort he has spared and for the detailed, precise comments he has provided.

Mr. P.J. Bishop, Librarian, Cardiothoracic Institute, Brompton Hospital, has provided me with much useful material on the stethoscope including a copy of his *Evolution of the Stethoscope*. I am in debt to Dr Alex Sakula, physician, Redhill General Hospital, Surrey, for bringing to my notice Dr Clark's interest in the stethoscope and for putting me in touch with Mme Galkowski, director of the Bibliothèque de l'Université de Nantes, who kindly supplied copies of two of Clark's letters to Laennec.

Mr. Murray Mindlin was a constant source of help and encouragement throughout the whole venture and I thank him warmly.

There are footnotes in the book, but I have tried to keep them to a minimum; they can be ignored with impunity and I hope without loss of interest or intelligibility. To reduce their number I have avoided giving precise references to well-known subjects; thus in quoting Keats's letters I have considered it sufficient to give the date and the recipient, and for these extracts I have used Gittings' *Letters of John Keats* OUP 1970; for other letters I have indicated their origin.

Anyone in any way familiar with the Keats's story will realise how heavily I have relied on the major biographies; three of these have been my constant guides - Aileen Ward, Dorothy Hewlett and Robert Gittings, whose wisdom and skill are a continuing source of inspiration.

Finally, I might add that anyone who reads this book and gets one tenth the pleasure that I have had in its preparation will indeed be happy.

H.S.
Whetstone and Dunwich, 1995.

CHAPTER I

Introduction

(i)

What can be said of John Keats that has not already been said? The libraries bulge with biographies and books, pamphlets and articles continue to proliferate on every aspect of his poetry, letters, development and psychology. And medicine? Purists may say that any such extraneous influence is irrelevant and that it is legitimate to judge Keats or indeed any other poet by his poetry alone; as he himself might have put it, that is all you know, and all you need to know. But as soon as we begin to look at the man as well as the poet, we must take into account early experiences and formative influences. Who can separate Shelley from his time at Oxford, Wordsworth from the Lake District or the Brontës from the Yorkshire moors? In Keats's case not only his training as a physician but also his tragic experience of tuberculosis in his family and personal life give medicine a particular relevance and importance which have probably been underestimated. Thus some may view medicine as purely an accidental encounter, an artefact of no consequence in the growth and eventual flowering of the genius of the poet John Keats, and this attitude is certainly represented in some of the biographies, particularly the early ones. Others do give medical influences a fair hearing, and there are a number of articles which treat specific medical problems in relation to Keats, most notably tuberculosis. In general terms however, it might be said that considering the volume that has been written about a man who died aged 25, having published his first poem at 21, but who spent six years of his life from the age of 16 training to be a doctor, an argument could be raised that medicine has not had a fair deal in the Keats debacle. What I have tried to do in this book is to examine the whole range of influences that medicine had on Keats's life and development, to seek clues linking his poetry with medicine, and to record how tuberculosis changed his life and eventually killed him.

I have had great difficulty in deciding into what category to place this book, for I wanted to avoid writing yet another biography of which there is no shortage. But how does one avoid biography in the telling of the medical story? Quite clearly this is impossible, and I have given such biographical details as I think essential to support the medical theme. Perhaps this is a medical biography, if there is such a thing; but the reader must decide. What follows for the remainder of this opening chapter is a review in chronological order of what others have done on the Keats-Medicine theme. I have approached this in two ways, looking at the major biographies for their medical content and then follows a closer examination of those publications which have dealt specifically with medical aspects of Keats's life and work. Information on different aspects of Keats's life is available in bewildering profusion but often fragmented in a large number of publications. I have therefore tried to bring this scattered information together, and where possible to make a coherent story against the medical background. Throughout I have tried to keep in mind developments in medicine with the result that medical history has had considerable importance in putting this story together.

(ii)

Keats does not lack biographies; without difficulty I have been able to trace a score or so[1] of major biographies in English, and there are at least another dozen 'lives' including three in French, two in Italian, one in German, one in Swedish and one in Japanese. I doubt if this is anything like a complete list. A fair number of works do not easily fall into categories and I have excluded from this list novels based on Keats's life and 'fictionalised' versions.

Keats died in 1821 and his first[2] published biography was by Richard Monckton Milnes, later Lord Houghton. This work came out in 1848, had a number of editions but all of them are singularly lacking in any medical content. Milnes had the advantage of a manuscript prepared by Charles Armitage Brown who had been a close friend of Keats when they shared a house together in Hampstead. Brown's own biography of Keats, delayed in publication until 1937, is marred by invective against those

---

[1] See Appendix II.
[2] I have excluded Leigh Hunt's inaccurate account based largely on Abbey's memories.

whom he considered responsible for his friend's untimely end. There are virtually no medical details but it is interesting to see how someone as close to Keats as Brown, even allowing for the state of medical knowledge at the time, is prepared to consider that tuberculosis was merely a factor contributing to his death. Brown summarises,

> After twenty years, with all the charity of which my nature is capable, my belief continues to be that he was destroyed by hirelings, under the imposing name of Reviewers. Consumption, it may be urged, was in the family; his father[3] and younger brother had both died of it, therefore his fate was inevitable.

In 1880 Frances M. Owen published her life of Keats and specifically states that despite five years preparation for medicine, the experience does not seem to have influenced him, 'it is strange how little trace we find of this work in his poems'. This is the first record I have been able to find of what I call the 'non-medical influence', an attitude adopted by a fair proportion of later biographies. I deal with Owen's opinion in more detail in Chapter IV.

In 1883 Harry Buxton Forman published *The poetical works and other writing of John Keats*. This is a major work with a great deal of supplementary material. Sir Benjamin Ward Richardson introducing this work in the *Asclepiad* in 1884 interprets a passage in Forman's biography regarding Keats's 1817 letter to his friend Bailey with whom he had recently been staying in Oxford. Richardson writes, 'in that visit (Keats) runs loose, pays a forfeit for his indiscretion which ever afterwards physically and morally embarrasses him'. This seems to be the origin of the implication that Keats may have had a venereal disease. (See Chapter VI.)

There is little of medical interest in William Michael Rossetti's life (1887) except perhaps to note that he accepts as speaking for itself Keats's comment in the letter to Bailey in 1817 that 'The little Mercury I have taken has corrected the poison ... though I feel ... I shall never again be secure in Robustness ...'. This passage from Bailey's letter has been the subject of much comment and some controversy by subsequent biographers. These have been largely resolved by Gittings. The subject is dealt with in detail in Chapter VI.

---

[3] Brown's memory is at fault; Keats's father died after a fall from his horse in 1804. See page 32.

Sir Sidney Colvin produced a number of works on Keats. The first edition of a small biography *Keats* appeared in 1887 and even in this small volume Colvin gives a fair amount of detail relating to Keats's apprenticeship with apothecary-surgeon Hammond, his time at Guy's Hospital and the final phase of his illness in Rome is described. Colvin's second biography *Life of John Keats*, published in 1917, is a full, mature assessment of the poet and his work, and the facts of medical training are well described as is the final illness. He contrasts Keats's training with that of other poets.

> The years between the sixteenth and twentieth of his age, are the most critical of a young man's life, and in these years, during which our other chief London-born poets Spenser, Milton, Gray, were profiting by the discipline of Cambridge and the Muses, Keats had no better or helpful regular training than that of an ordinary apprentice, apparently one of several, in a suburban surgery.

But even Colvin who wrote so sympathetically and knowledgeably about the inspiration and influences of literature and art in Keats's work, summarised his attitude to medicine in what is a verbatim quote from Benjamin Ward Richardson:

> He never attached much consequence to his own studies in medicine, and indeed looked upon the medical career as the career by which to live in a workaday world, without being certain he could keep up with the strain of it.

The first major American biography of Keats by Amy Lowell appeared in 1925. This is a detailed two volume work, flamboyant, perhaps a little dramatised. We are informed that 'Mr Hammond kept two apprentices...'. In Volume II we read 'He had pulmonary tuberculosis and laryngeal tuberculosis', and the author refers the reader to Volume I when she quotes the opinion of Dr John B. Hawes II - a specialist in tuberculosis at the Massachusetts General Hospital - on the health history of Keats produced by Miss Lowell. Dr Hawes states:

> ... it is not inconsistent with pulmonary tuberculosis and laryngeal tuberculosis. Although not typical of the latter, I have seen not a few cases of laryngeal tuberculosis that have acted in just the way this one has done ...

Lowell also suggests that the start of Keats's tuberculosis should be dated from autumn 1817, not as usually from the Scottish walking holiday in August 1819. She also enters the venereal disease controversy. These speculations on medical topics in this biography may not be entirely unjustified but they cannot be substantiated either.

A translation from the French of Albert Erlande's book on Keats was published in English in 1929. There are no particular medical 'insights' but there is the interesting comment that Keats laid bare his sufferings in his works after the manner of Musset.

Ifor Evans produced a book of 143 pages in 1934. This is a delightful volume, elegantly written and there is one passage which expresses a view of the medicine/poetry relationship in Keats which approximates to my own.

> Medicine never came into his poetry; the realism that enters from close contact with the physical world, with the body, its flesh and putrefactions, and the bright, clean hardness of bones, is all removed from his iridescent verse. His practical life came into being in these years of medical study, but it was a thing apart, stolen pleasure.

Dorothy Hewlett published the first version of her life of Keats in 1937 and this I think, is a watershed in regards to Keats's biographies. Not only is this a factual and sympathetic account of the life, but there are fine interpretations of Keats's self-argument and its resolution in poetry particularly in *Endymion*: I have more to say on this later. Medicine, whether it be Keats's training, the manner in which it influenced his life or the effects of tuberculosis, are all given detailed coverage. This work marks a new phase in which the modern biographer dissects the subject in detail and often with great skill showing the complex influences that weave the fabric of life. One important strand in the fabric of Keats's life is shown to be medicine, and this is perhaps the first time the subject is given its due in a major biography of the poet.

A number of works published in the 1940's and '50's add little to known facts, and provide no special medical interest. Betty Askwith's (1941) book comes in this category, so does the elegant little pamphlet written by Edmund Blunden for the British Council and published in 1950. Guy Murchie's *The spirit of the place in Keats* (1955), gives good descriptions of Keats's physical appearance, mentions Hammond's two apprentices but is otherwise not concerned with medicine. In the 1960's came three works from the United States - Ward (1963), Bate (1963) and Bush (1966). The latter by Professor Douglas Bush of Harvard is a brief critical biography. Aileen Ward's book is a most accomplished scholarly work with the sub-title, *The making of a poet*. In her preface Miss Ward states:

> Where his previous biographers have viewed him against the long tradition of English poetry or his day-to-day study of the poets from whom he learned his art ... I have tried to convey something of the inner drama of his creative life as it is recorded in his poems and letters.

This is a most convincing study of Keats, treading carefully between, on one hand the dangers of speculation and the paucity of facts on the other, in which a balanced compromise is presented. This is well demonstrated in the detailed discussion - probably the fullest coverage in any general biography up to the date of this publication - of Keats's apparent change in direction when he became apprenticed to Hammond. Other medical matters are also given full coverage.

Walter Jackson Bate, another distinguished American, produced a standard critical biography in which the medical facts of Keats's life are fairly treated (a whole chapter is given to the Guy's period) but there are no particular medical insights and no discussion on the possible medical influences in the poems.

Taken somewhat out of chronological order, two other books deserve comment. First, *A Doctor's Life of John Keats* by Walter A. Wells, published in 1959, is a short account of the life, written in a rather romantic colloquial style. It is a strange mixture of biography, at times fictionalised, comment on medical treatment and ending with a short essay on the mystery of Genius. The book is written primarily for non-medical readers. Dr Wells has one firm conclusion namely that the 'little mercury' Keats was taking had nothing to do with syphilis.

In 1967 Jean Haynes produced a small book - *The Young Keats* - which is a 'fictionalised' account of his early life. The author however, does give the name 'Hodge' to Hammond's 'second apprentice'. As will be seen from Chapter III I have been unable to substantiate that there was in fact a second apprentice, never mind being able to identify him by name. Having had the advantage of discussing this matter with Mrs Haynes, I have to report that the name Hodge given to the second apprentice is entirely her own invention.

Robert Gittings gave us his *John Keats* in 1968 - a detailed biography of some 450 pages - fully documented and presented with great skill and energy. Mr Gittings had already produced a number of publications on selected aspects of Keats, including medical aspects (some to be examined later), but this full biography is the epitome of his knowledge and research into all facets of Keats's life. Because of the great detail and abundant references, the text is at times turgid and difficult to read, but anyone seeking facts, or opinions based on well deduced arguments, will find no better work to consult. This is certainly true of the medical aspects of Keats's life. We owe Mr Gittings a debt of gratitude for he has reclaimed some of the prestige in erudition and scholarship for Keats's own country which had moved across the Atlantic following a wave of great American biographies and other publications on Keats. Barring the uncovering of many new facts or revelations in documents, both unlikely suppositions, it is difficult to see Gittings' life being superseded.

In this bicentenary year, 1995, Stephen Coote has published his *John Keats*. This full length biography goes over well trodden ground, but emphasizes an aspect of Keats's character which might be called his social conscience. By tracing Keats's reaction and distaste for conditions in early 19th century England Keats emerges, not perhaps as fully politically conscious as Shelley, but nevertheless, a lively critic of contemporary church and state.

In dealing with medicine in Keats's life Coote favours the view that he took up this profession as a result of the profound experience of his mother's death. The idea is developed that poetry became a reaction from the experience of hospital life, as Coote puts it 'Poetry is a consolation for the horrors of real life'. Apollo, we are told comes to be seen as the god of medicine as well as poetry, soothing body as well as mind. If this proposition is valid at all it is only so in the early phase of Keats's life, in the Cowden Clarke Hammond stage. It can hardly be maintained for the end of his medical training, at the time of his 'I mean to rely on my Abilities as a Poet' confrontation with Abbey.

This short review of Keats's major biographies indicates that there has continued to be a fairly consistent interest in Keats's life and work. With the exceptions of Colvin and Buxton Forman however, the facts of Keats's medical life are given scant attention until well into the 20th century. Lowell certainly gave the facts and added controversy but it was not until 1937 that Hewlett gave not only the facts of Keats's medical life but discussed in detail the relationship between medicine and poetry. A growing realisation of the position occupied by medicine in Keats's life is shown by later biographers, particularly Ward and culminating in Gittings' detailed life; both of these biographers make good use of the specialist medicine publications largely ignored by earlier writers.

(iii)

More specialised treatment of medical themes have usually taken the form of short articles, printed lectures or pamphlets; several have been bound in book form but even Hale-White who provided perhaps the most ambitious early attempt to come to terms with Keats and medicine does so in less than 100 pages. Unlike the main biographies - often tomes of several volumes - the 'medical evidence' is to be found by perusal of 'slender volumes'.

In terms of chronological order and considerable general significance, first mention must go to Sir Benjamin Ward Richardson who produced in the *Asclepiad* of April 1884 an article entitled *An Aesculapian Poet - John Keats*. Richardson's paper is in fact a combination of conversations he had with Henry Stephens, a medical student friend of Keats, together with an introduction or commentary on the recently published work of Harry Buxton Forman. Richardson gives a resumé of the life in a full-blooded even brusque but friendly manner. His view on Severn for instance:

> Of all the friends who noticed Keats, from genial Hunt to sublime Shelley; of all the hands that helped him, not excluding George Keats, his brother, and the Brawnes, no friend was the like of Severn. It is a real happiness to know that the world does sometimes, by some good fortune, possess such a nature of love and constancy.

Of some importance are the recollections of Stephens as told by Richardson. Here for instance is the origin of the, 'A thing of beauty' anecdote which finds a place in most studies of Keats.

Richardson has an interesting aside on the medicine versus poetry conflict:

> It has been said that Keats, although educated for our own profession of medicine, had no talent for it. In that vulgar acceptance

of the term, which converts talent into success as tested by the money-getting standard, the height and splendour of the idol of the market-place, that may be true. It requires an immense amount of inborn stupidity and withering of heart, and lowering of soul, and worship of dumb ugliness, to secure success in the money market of a profession, which in its purity is too exalted for wealth either to nourish or debase. But if Keats had once tasted the true spirit of medicine, he would I believe, have become one of her greatest sons - an addition perchance, to the some eight or ten of the men of all time whom medicine claims as her own, her poets of nature, like Keats himself, and in their way poetising in undying thoughts if not in measured lines.

A similar view was later to be expressed by Dorothy Hewlett. Richardson quotes the passage in the letter to Taylor in which Keats speculates on the usefulness of occupation in maintaining good health in city dwellers. 'Our health, temperament, disposition are taken more from the air we breathe than is generally imagined.' This is an important concept in the origin of mental disorder and having quoted the passage Richardson concludes 'Keats not a physician! why, the father of physic himself might have written what the poet has here indited'. The contrast between this view of Keats and that of Owen is startling: an explanation could lie in the fact that in 1880 when Owen published her life she almost certainly did not have access to Keats's letters which appeared three years later with the Buxton Forman volumes reviewed by Richardson in his article in the *Asclepiad*. And Richardson, himself a medical man, must have been more receptive and sympathetic to medical nuances. Certainly at a relatively early date in the history of Keats's biographies he set a strikingly original trend not necessarily accepted by those who followed, medical men or not.

There is a little known paper in the Westminster Review of 1907 by the South African Louis Leipoldt entitled *John Keats, Medical Student*. The author, introducing his subject complains that at the time of writing there was no full and exhaustive life of Keats and that despite Forman's edition of the letters, the early years of Keats's life remain a mystery. The author then gives a brief summary of Keats's apprenticeship to Hammond and describes his hospital life at Guy's. He criticises Richardson for assuming that it was Hammond's ill-treatment of his apprentice which gave Keats his distaste for the profession he had chosen. Leipoldt is perhaps the first to take a close look at the possible way in which medicine might have impinged on the poet's writing; the relative inaccessibility of this paper may be responsible for its apparent lack of influence on others who have shown interest in the medical aspects of Keats's life and work. The following passages taken from Leipoldt's paper give the substance of his views.

> As a matter of fact, no one, unacquainted with the details of his hospital career, would be able to say, from the mere study of his poetry, that Keats ever possessed any medical training or knew anything whatever of medical science. He was sufficiently an artist to discount the mere morbid sentimentality of the doctor's trade. He had penetrated too far into the Temple of Disease, both as acolyte and victim, to take delight in impressing on the outside public the beauty and the agony of what he had witnessed. Those who stood on the threshold like Coleridge and Shelley, could sing of the sentiment underlying it all, and make artistic copy out of the gruesome. He, the initiate, had lost his inquisitiveness when he had learned to appreciate the truth.
>
> He had learnt, early enough, to see morbid things in their true perspective, unblurred by any haze of false shame or a halo of sickly sentimentality. But it is possible that he distrusted himself to speak of things he had seen during his hospital days.
>
> It is for this reason that one finds so little in his works that is of direct bearing upon his position as a medical student. Dr Richardson, who has called him the "Aesculapian Singer" found nothing which could not equally well have been penned by a layman ignorant of the veriest rudiments of leechcraft. That in itself proves nothing. It is not by the definite expressions in his poems, so much as by the general character of the whole of his works, that one can find justification for the statement that his medical career did influence him.

This last sentence is the most balanced and mature judgement on the manner in which Keats's medical experience influenced his work. I say this although I do not completely agree, for I hope to show later that there are in fact a number of direct statements of definite expressions as Leipoldt calls them, to be found in the poems. It is surprising that these views, available for the past three quarters of a century, have had so little influence on subsequent work. Leipoldt finishes his paper by finding Keats 'less Aesculapian than the enthusiastic Dr Richardson imagined him to be ... but one who appeals as much to the general reader as to the medical man'.

There follows a period of 14 years in which nothing of medical interest was published on Keats until in 1921 Sir George Newman produced a lecture in printed form dedicated to the Master of the Society of Apothecaries of London for the centenary year of Keats's death. Sir George entitles his 36-page lecture *John Keats Apothecary and Poet*, emphasises the period of early medical training, and summarises his view on the part played by this training on the poet:

> It is impossible to believe that a medical training of six years had left no enduring effect on a sensitive and responsive mind like John Keats. Can the study of Medicine leave a man where it finds him? Whether he practices his profession or not, is he not marked for life?

He finds what he calls a 'subtle touch of deterrence in the hospital patient' in *Hyperion* -

> As with us mortal men, the laden heart
> Is persecuted more, and fever'd more,
> When it is nighing to the mournful house
> Where other hearts are sick of the same bruise.

Sir George quotes Rossetti and Matthew Arnold as placing Keats with Shakespeare and also Colvin's view that '... he was the most Shakespearean spirit that has lived since Shakespeare'. Into this short lecture Sir George has fitted a good many of the facts of Keats's life and training and has condensed many views of the poet in a most skilful and entertaining manner.

In the Guy's Hospital Gazette in 1925 appeared a short article entitled *Keats at Guy's* by Alfred G. Harris, quoting the same journal for 1905 in which the name 'Junkets' is given as the nickname applied to Keats while at Guy's. Harris also comments that Keats 'deserts Aesculapius for Apollo'.

Guy's again comes to the fore with the publication by Sir William Hale-White's *Keats as doctor and patient* in 1938. This is an expansion of the author's previously published article entitled *Keats as a medical student* which appeared in Guy's Hospital Reports for July 1925. In the expanded work Hale-White gives good biographical details and fills in the historical background emphasising the Guy's-Thomas's axis. About the apprenticeship period he mentions specifically that Hammond had two apprentices: 'Hammond kept two apprentices, so that Keats had time for reading and he appears to have been happy'. This appears to be no more than the conventional interpretation of Colvin's account of the apprenticeship. Hale-White deals with the venereal disease episode but Gittings feels that Hale-White discussed the matter as if the only possible diagnosis was syphilis whereas the differential diagnosis in Gittings' view, should include other venereal diseases. A nice lesson from the lay for the medical practitioner. The subject is dealt with in detail in Chapter VI.

Leaving aside the venereal disease controversy and the details of Keats's tuberculosis, Hale-White is disappointing in his lack of any mention of the broader aspects of medical influence and one misses the acute observations of Richardson, Leipoldt and Newman. There is for instance no comment on why Keats took up medicine. Hale-White seems content to record the facts. It will therefore come as no surprise that in his summing up in the final words of his book Hale-White writes:

> It is clear that his medical studies influenced his writing so little as to be negligible. This is remarkable, for although he had for five years out of his short life studied medicine and had been in daily contact with possible medical subjects for writing, he did not use them. His natural industry made him work hard at medicine but his mind was not in it.

After 1938 although a number of biographies were published indicating no lack of interest in Keats, specific medical topics go unmentioned until 1969 when C.T. Andrews produced his article on *Keats and Mercury*. This paper gives a history of the medical use of mercury and goes over the syphilis controversy opened up by Lowell. Even with the benefit of Gittings' appendix on the subject (see Chapter VI), Andrews concludes cautiously '... the evidence available so far does not support the diagnosis of venereal disease and to suggest that judgement on this issue be suspended unless or until new facts emerge'.

For the 150th anniversary of Keats's death Robert Gittings entitled his paper in *Contemporary Review* of Sept. 1971 *Keats and Medicine*. This

---

[4] See: G. Hamilton-Edwards. Letter to *T.L.S.* 28th March 1968.

short article of five pages is full of interest and it is disappointing that some of the themes touched upon could not be explored in more detail. There is for instance the revelation[4] that members of the Hammond family were given to habitual drunkenness and the suggestion that this may have had something to do with Keats's quarrel with his master.

The question is raised of why Keats never practiced as a doctor. Gittings makes the point that to answer this we must distinguish between Keats as a physician and Keats as a surgeon. This seems to me an extremely important point for one can trace Keats's distaste for things surgical, sometimes openly expressed, but he does not come forward in condemning the physician's life. Clearly if he had practiced medicine he would have carried a stethoscope rather than wielded the knife. Gittings points out that he was expected, having obtained the L.S.A., to go on to take the M.R.C.S. - a surgical qualification. But we are still left wondering why he did not practice as a physician.

The Sydenham lecture given on the 150th anniversary of Keats's death was delivered by Lord Brock before the Faculty of the History of Medicine of the Society of Apothecaries. The lecture, published in 1973 is entitled *John Keats and Joseph Severn: The Tragedy of the Last Illness*. Lord Brock - a distinguished surgeon and a Guy's man had already shown interest in the relation between medicine and literature in his article in 1925 in the Guy's Hospital Gazette entitled *Medical Men in Literature*.

In his Sydenham lecture Lord Brock states that despite Lady Birkenhead's two published accounts of Severn's devotion to Keats in the last phases of his illness, the details are not sufficiently well known. He also complains that Gittings in his biography presents this aspect of the life scantily and does not give Severn sufficient credit. A rereading of Gittings indicates that it is difficult to see how such an argument can be sustained.

Brock compliments Hale-White on his monograph on Keats in which he gives what Brock calls the only medical presentation of Keats's consumption. This is in fact not quite correct for in 1955 Anthony J. Daly produced a paper in the Medical Press entitled *A notable case of pulmonary Tuberculosis*. This article in a somewhat obscure journal attributes to Keats the quotation 'Poetry, is the only thing worth the attention of superior minds, and compared to it all other pursuits are mean and tame'. It is easy to see that this could be used to indicate Keats's preference for poetry rather than medicine.

In his lecture Brock gives a brief history of tuberculosis, its treatment and deals in detail with Keats's tuberculosis. He states that there can be no reasonable doubt that John acquired his infection from his brother Tom who died from the disease in December 1818. Brock looks carefully into the possibility that Keats's recurrent 'sore throats' might have been a manifestation of tuberculosis either of the pharynx or larynx, and concludes that there is insufficient evidence to support either diagnosis. He also makes the interesting observation that in reviewing Keats's own attitude to his illness, Keats seems to have accepted it as a development in his general unfitness, and that he did not treat it as if it were entirely unsuspected.

Brock, with surgical pragmatism considers that Dr Clark, who looked after Keats in Rome, gave a very poor assessment of Keats's illness, even allowing for the state of medical knowledge in 1820. He is however, quite fair in his treatment of Clark and considers that he may have improved as a doctor in later life.

The lecture ends with mention of whether Keats intended his epitaph to read 'Here lies one whose name was writ in water' or 'on water'. Brock also gives evidence of Severn's devotion to his friend.

Before concluding this section dealing with publications that have dealt specifically with selected aspects of Keats and medicine, some mention must be made of Professor Stuart Sperry's work (1973). Rather than looking for direct references or clues that might give away the poet's medical training, Sperry raises interesting points on Keats's use of language in relation to his scientific training, particularly his knowledge of chemistry. He develops this in relation to Keats's use of 'sensation' and I refer again to this in Chapter IV. Sperry's observation is a nice subtlety which might be considered an extension of the view expressed by Leipoldt that the key to medical influences in Keats's work lie not so much in definite expressions but in 'the general character of his whole works ...'.

A major extension of Sperry's initiative is to be found in the work of D.C. Goellnicht whose, *The Poet - Physician* appeared in 1984. This is a detailed scholarly study, by far the most ambitious and successful work published[5] on the Keats and medicine theme. In his introduction Goellnicht

---

[5] In his review of previous work on Keats and Medicine Goellnicht states that, 'the first and only full-length study of Keats's medical training by a literary critic is Charles Hagelman's doctoral dissertation'; he quotes extensively from it. This is an unpublished Ph.D dissertation from the University of Texas, Austin dated 1956 and has not been available to this author. G. states that much of the information in the thesis appeared in Aileen Wards, *John Keats - The Making of a Poet*.

states, 'This book examines the influence of Keats's medical training and knowledge on his poems and letters, an influence that has usually been ignored or denied'. The author does just that, and more, for he extends the medical influence to include all the components of Keats's medical curriculum including chemistry, botany, anatomy, physiology, pathology and medicine. Appropriately, Goellnicht subtitles his book, *Keats and Medical Science*. We are given therefore a comprehensive, indeed exhaustive coverage of the subject. By extending Sperry's approach of Keats's use of language in relation to chemistry, Goellnicht with great skill, and very detailed knowledge of the works, finds multiple allusions, not only in physical events but in psychological nuances, tracing word-meanings to a whole variety of Keats's scientific training or observations and linking these to specific points in Keats's poems. If previously one complained that there was a lack of medical influences in the works, Goellnicht now provides an abundance, if not an excess. The difficulty with this method, despite the author's undoubted skill and innovation, is that the allusion, or linkage between science and poem is made in such detail that the result may appear tenuous or even unbelievable.

In Chapter IV (page 62) I quote Goodall's comments on Keats's use of the word 'blood' at the end of *Endymion Book IV* - 'And warm with dew at ooze from living blood'. Goellnicht goes much further than Goodall and puts his view that what Keats really had in mind was serum, which separates or oozes when blood clots. Who can say if this is justified?

Another example of Goellnicht's rather contrived references is the way in which Keats is said in various letters to describe the phenomenon of poetic creation as likened to a frenzied fever. This reference is true enough, but whether it can be ascribed to Keats's medical training is at best doubtful.

Despite these criticisms of special pleading, or overegging the pudding, Goellnicht's book is a *tour de force*, scholarly, accurate, courageous.

CHAPTER II

Early Life

Edmonton is a suburb of north London; it forms part of an area in what was the county of Middlesex, crowded with houses and cluttered with industrial and commercial works. The suburb today is a northern extension of London resulting from 19th century expansion when many of the villages and small towns surrounding the capital were linked by new forms of transport - particularly the railways. Houses, more houses, people and factories fill the gaps between roads and green spaces.

Robinsons's history of Edmonton published in 1819 admonishes the reader -

> In reviewing the topographical recommendations of the parish of Edmonton, it might reasonably be presumed, even if documents had been wanting to establish the fact, that a place possessing so many local advantages, the beauty of the scenery, the variety of the views, and its vicinity to the metropolis, would not be over-looked by those whose rank and fortune enabled them to select a suitable residence. It accordingly became from the earliest periods, the residence of those whose opulence and taste adorned it with mansions adapted to their dignity and station. These indeed, have long since so entirely disappeared as to leave nothing behind them but the name.

A good deal of destruction by fire during the Second World War, followed by housing development schemes often with small skyscraper concrete blocks of flats, completes the present-day picture of a somewhat grim industrial London suburb barely distinguishable from a multitude of others. The modern reader and no doubt motorist, is most likely to know the area because he is able to enter and also to leave it by way of a section of the North Circular Road, the best known part of which is Silver Street.

At the beginning of the 19th century the population of England, Wales and Scotland numbered perhaps 11 millions, one million of whom resided in London. It was a period of rapid growth of industrial cities with a shift of population away from the land into the cities, encouraged by factory wages and the lack of common land as a direct result of the Enclosure Acts at the end of the 18th century.

England, though an island, was not immune from political and philosophical movements in Continental Europe. The vanguard of continental enlightenment spearheaded by the *philosophes* Rousseau and Voltaire prepared the ground for the upheaval of the French revolution while in England, an Irishman - Burke - preferred to consider the French experience as a particular example of a phenomenon which he recognised as being general, in his *Reflections on the Revolution in France*. The subsequent domination of Europe by Napoleon made continental travel impossible or at best extremely hazardous; what amounted to a mutual blockade of British and continental ports by the navies of the adversaries produced almost siege conditions - exchange of goods and commodities almost ceased. Cognac, for instance, the gentleman's drink, was almost completely supplanted by Scotch whisky - a trend not altogether reversed even to this day.

In mid-summer 1805, with Bonaparte controlling large areas of Europe, there came to live in Edmonton an unusual family; unusual because it consisted of a grandmother and four young children. The grandmother, Mrs Alice Jennings, recently widowed, brought with her John aged 10, George aged 8, Tom aged 7 and Frances Mary aged 2 - the four children of her daughter Frances.

Alice Jennings' husband, John, had been a successful innkeeper who ran the Swan and Hoop livery stables in Moorgate - a busy, bustling establishment providing 'bait' or refreshment for travellers - often businessmen driving from north London to the city. Here Frances Jennings grew up and, as the innkeeper's daughter naturally came into contact with those frequenting the inn and those employed there. Among the latter was a young man called Thomas Keats, probably from the West Country, who was first employed as an ostler but by the age of 20 Thomas was head groom at the Swan and Hoop. Little is known of Thomas Keats's origin, but the similarity between the name Keats and that of Keate belonging to a large family group well know in the West Country, offers some evidence that John Keats's father came from that part of England. In later life John never spoke or wrote about his father.

Frances Jennings, Keats's mother, had been brought up in a manner befitting a successful innkeeper's daughter, with a fair degree of comfort or even affluence. Her brothers, Midgley John and Thomas, went to Clarke's School at Enfield, but it is not known how she was educated. At the age of 19 Frances was a tall, good-looking girl - 'a lively woman' - and if we are to accept the account of Abbey, subsequently Keats's guardian, she was keen on displaying her good legs by lifting her skirts more than she need do when crossing muddy streets. (It is suggested that she preferred walking out in bad weather, for this gave her better opportunity of displaying her legs.)

A more accurate assessment of Frances comes from George Keats writing to Dilke in 1825:

> My mother I distinctly remember, she resembled John very much in the Face was extremely fond of him and humoured him in every whim, of which he had not a few, she was a most excellent and affectionate parent and as I thought a woman of uncommon talents, she was confined to her bed for many years by a rheumatism and at last died of a Consumption, she would have sent us to Harrow school as I often heard say, if she could have afforded.[6]

No information is available about the courtship of the young pair, but we do know that Thomas Keats and Frances Jennings were married in St. George's, Hanover Square on October 9th 1794; their first son John was born on 31st October 1795. Two other sons followed, George in 1797, Tom in 1799 and a daughter, Frances Mary was born in 1803. A fourth boy, Edward, was born in April 1801 but died in December of the following year.

We have few precise details of Keats's very early years; when learning to talk he would not only echo the last word said but would give it a rhyme; he had something of a violent nature - when aged perhaps five there is the story that when his mother was ill and absolute quiet was ordered, he kept guard on her door with an old sword, allowing no one to enter. Another version of this story has it that John got hold of a sword and kept his mother prisoner in the house. Whichever version one accepts, John in fact, had a close relationship with his mother, according to his brother, and 'humoured him in every whim, of which he had not a few'.

---

[6] See Lowell I p.13. (Original letter in Lowell's collection).

In 1803 when John was about eight, he and his brother George were sent to a school in Enfield run by John Clarke. This was probably the first major identifiable good fortune that befell John Keats. His mother, it seems, had ideas of sending him to Harrow and who would speculate on the possible outcome if her apparent wishes had been fulfilled, but we do know, particularly from the writings of John Clarke's son Charles Cowden, the pattern and many details of Keats's school life in Enfield.

The school building was a fine one, dating from *c*.1670, built it is said, for a West India merchant. It was situated in the village of Enfield, surrounded by meadows and wooded estates on the New River where the boys bathed.

John Clarke the headmaster, was a progressive man with liberal views both in politics and in education. He took *The Examiner* - a leftish weekly edited by Leigh Hunt; both the paper and its editor had an important influence in Keats's later development. At a time when flogging in schools was commonplace, Clarke substituted a scheme of bad and good marks, encouraging the latter with prizes. There was an excellent school library full of history and geography; French was taught and Keats learned to read the language.

The seventy or eighty boys lived in a community, not excessively authoritarian, in which a degree of individuality was encouraged and in every aspect of which the benign prudence of John Clarke was discernible. Here young Keats had his first lessons from Charles Cowden Clarke, son of the headmaster, who was then aged 14 or 15, and Keats lived the life of an aggressive schoolboy more interested in fighting than in books. As a contemporary Edward Holmes, put it -

> He was a boy whom any one, from his extraordinary vivacity and personal beauty, might easily have fancied would become great - but rather in some military capacity than in literature.

From time to time the Keats boys were visited by their parents who would drive out to Enfield in a gig driven by their father. On one tragic weekend Thomas Keats rode alone on horseback, and he was by all accounts a good horseman, to visit his sons at school. When he left them he may well have called on friends in nearby Southgate. On his way back to the city he fell from his horse and was killed. *The Times* of Tuesday, April 17th, 1804 reported -

> On Sunday, Mr Keats, livery-stable keeper in Moorfields, went to

dine at Southgate; he returned at a late hour, and on passing down the City-road, his horse fell with him, when he had the misfortune to fracture his skull. It was about one o'clock in the morning when the watchman found him, he was at that time alive but speechless; the watchman got assistance and took him to a house in the neighbourhood, where he died about eight o'clock.

Thomas Keats, aged thirty, died intestate, leaving his wife Frances, aged twenty-nine, with three boys and a baby girl. His widow eventually inherited rather less than £2,000. These facts may have had something to do with Frances' hasty remarriage, for just over two months after Thomas Keats's death, Frances married William Rawlings, who has been described as a bank clerk.

We do not know what effect his father's death had on the ten-year old schoolboy; children of this age will often recollect such events with ease in later life but they assimilate such knowledge over a period of time as if a gestation period is required for full comprehension of the facts. Neither is it clear how much contact there was between William and Frances Rawlings and the Keats children - Fanny Keats in later life said 'My brothers and myself never lived with them but always with my grandmother'.

Misfortune continued, for in March 1805 grandfather Jennings died; he left a sum of £13,000 but his will was contested by his daughter Frances. The marriage between Frances and Rawlings was not a success; by 1806 William Rawlings was living alone at the Swan and Hoop and his wife had left him. At this time Frances Rawlings seems to have disappeared or at least to have kept a sufficiently low profile to avoid precise records of her movements. Estranged from her mother due to the contest over her father's will, and without money, it may be that she was living with another man - although there is no more than hearsay evidence for this. Rawlings stayed on at the Swan and Hoop for several years but is lost sight of after 1808. He does not seem to have accepted any responsibility for his step-children.

These vicissitudes in the adult world around him following the sudden death of his father, his mother's remarriage and subsequent disappearance together with family acrimony over his grandfather's contested will, had probably little major direct effect on the schoolboy Keats, but it might have been the source of his subsequent comment reported by Severn, 'Keats used to say that his great misfortune had been that from his infancy he had no mother'.

We can only conjecture at the effect of these circumstances on the young Keats, but we are in no doubt on one consequence of this turmoil; his grandmother took charge of the children. Alice Jennings, a farmer's daughter who understood children, and a Lancashire woman of character, took her four grandchildren to live at Ponders End and after the death of her husband moved to nearby Edmonton. John Jennings had suffered from gout and in his final illness his medical attendant was one Thomas Hammond of Edmonton. Hammond practised from his home in Church Street, Edmonton, and it was to this same street close to the doctor's house, that Mrs Jennings moved with her four grandchildren in midsummer 1805.

By the terms of John Jennings' will about half his fortune was to go to his wife, about one-third to his son and the rest to provide annuities of £50 and £30 respectively for his daughter and sister. A sum of £1,000 was to be divided among the Keats children.

In her court action against her mother and brother - the main executors - Frances claimed that she had been kept in ignorance of the contents of the will, that the executors had managed the will to their own advantage and had denied her possession of her rightful legacy of £50 per annum. The case was eventually heard in 1806 and was a complete vindication of the trustees' management. Frances' action failed. This complicated will, accountable to Chancery, was largely administered by Midgley John Jennings. Midgley John, lieutenant in the navy, died from tuberculosis just over two years after the court hearing, and one of his last acts was, by Order of Chancery, to pay his sister Frances' annuity arrears. This seems to have led to something of a reconciliation; at all events Frances reappeared and was accepted into her mother's house. However, Frances was now not well and took to her bed for long periods suffering from what her son George later called 'rheumatism'.

The home provided by their grandmother gave the Keats children some stable background but the lack of his mother's presence may well have been the source of John's violent behaviour during this period of his schooling. John was now 13, given to all the boyish pranks which he indulged in with more than ordinary zeal. During this period he appears as a headstrong, perverse fellow, not in the least willing to please his masters and barely scraping through his lessons. On one occasion, when Tom was cuffed by one of the junior masters for some misdemeanour, John rushed up to the master and struck him. John Clarke, the headmaster, dealt gently with this offence.

The return of his mother, now dependent and ill, seems to have rekindled all John's affection, while on her part Frances was indulgent and approving of all her eldest son's actions.

At the start of the new term in January 1809, John resolved to mend his ways. It is not clear what prompted this turning of a new leaf, but he set to work with the immediate object of entering for and taking the school prizes in literature. This 'overcompensation' meant that John got up earlier than anyone else to start his reading; he read through school meals; if ordered to take exercise he read while walking. In this way he read through the whole school library. The descriptions left by Cowden Clarke of this period have almost an implication that the young Keats was not only interested in acquiring knowledge but also of being seen to acquire knowledge. In any event his efforts were successful and in midsummer 1809 John Keats took first prize for translations from Latin and French - work done voluntarily in his spare time. This success and its subsequent repetition on many occasions, must surely be one of the major turning points in Keats's intellectual development. It was probably much more than this, for the immediate attainment of his prize - the result of sustained intellectual effort - demonstrated how his passionate energies could best be put to use, but in the longer term it laid the foundation of a knowledge of and an interest in the classics which was later to find such dominant expression in his poetry. During this time of intense adolescent hyperactivity, the direction of Keats's life was set, although the particular way in which his genius would manifest was not yet apparent.

In 1809 his prize was Kauffman's *Dictionary of Merchandise* and he was awarded the new edition of John Bonnycastle's *Introduction to Astronomy*. At this time Keats was reading French and Latin authors - translating Findon and Virgil and showed interest in Greek myths. Books which had a particular relevance include Andrew Tooke's *Pantheon*, the *Polymetis* of Joseph Spence and the *Bibliotheca Classica* of John Lemprière.

About this time Keats's mother died. Home from school for Christmas 1809, Keats found his mother seriously ill; it has always been assumed that she died from tuberculosis. John appointed himself custodian of his mother, allowing nobody but himself to administer Hammond's medicines. He cooked for her and sat up long hours at night reading to her.

This seems to have completed the transformation from wild schoolboy to contemplative student and voracious reader. He was subject to bouts of depression - 'hypochondriasm' according to George. The pressures of adolescence and the realities of life were beginning to make themselves felt.

Grandmother Jennings was now nearly seventy-five and needed help after her daughter's death in the upbringing of the Keats children. She appointed two guardians, Sandell and Abbey, to hold in trust the bequest from her husband to the children. Sandell had a minor role in these affairs, but Richard Abbey had an important function and probably some influence on the way in which John Keats's early life developed and on the management of the financial affairs of the other Keats children.

Abbey came from the same Lancashire village as Mrs Jennings and was a minor pillar of the eighteenth century English establishment. A prosperous tea broker, churchwarden, member of the Port of London Committee and Honourable Company of Girdlers, twice master of the Honourable Company of Pattern Makers and so on. The picture is almost Pickwickian, but Richard Abbey was prudent, shrewd, conscientious and a little malicious.

George Keats accepted Abbey's suggestion that he enter his counting house; a similar chance may have been offered to John, but tea brokerage was not for him. What else was open to the young Keats? His small stature made a career in the army unlikely, a lawyer perhaps but the law does not seem to have attracted young John. One would think that with his bookish nature and influenced by his friend Cowden Clarke, he was cut out to be a school teacher. With his contemplative nature and obsession with the classics, it is difficult to see him choosing a career which did not take into account these striking attributes. What could be more fitting than school teaching for a young man of modest means? And yet he decided to become a doctor. This last sentence - apparently so straightforward, yet replete with paradox, inconsistency and incomprehension - is the main reason for writing this book.

His chief biographers pay some attention to this extraordinary change in direction. There is controversy as to whether the decision to become a doctor was Keats's own or whether it resulted from Abbey's pressures. It is impossible to be certain - all we can do is look at the facts: John set out to be a doctor and succeeded; his own decision or not, it may well have been a compromise between what he did *not* want to do and what he thought he could do, while he was making up his mind what he must do.

CHAPTER III

Why Medicine
(i) The Decision

Unfortunately we do not have Keats's own statement on the reasons for his sudden change from arts to science. Certainly, we have no record that the decision was forced upon him; inherent in most discussion on this aspect of Keats's life is the implication that Abbey may have pushed him into medicine, but the record does not support any such action by his guardian. Cowden Clarke in his *Recollections of Keats* considers that medicine was 'his own selection' but also comments that 'He made no secret however, that he could not sympathise with the science of anatomy as a main pursuit in life'.

This, of course, refers to a later phase of Keats's medical education when the original decision had been long taken. Besides, he was not the first nor indeed the last medical student to find anatomy as the main pursuit in life a trifle disenchanting. Clarke also refers to the 'profession that had been chosen for him', lending some credence to the view that the choice of medicine was not Keats's own.

In any event medicine it was to be, and considered in the light of all available evidence, it does seem somewhat extraordinary, almost incomprehensible, that such an abrupt turn-about in activities should have been contemplated. Was he about to enter upon what Christopher Ricks has called 'the false start in medicine'.[7]

Anyone who has sons or daughters studying in the later stages of schooling, will be aware of the heart-searching which goes on in our own lives at that awkward time when we force our young to decide arts or science, and make it so difficult for them to reconsider or change direction one way or another. Suppose your son comes to you and says that he has achieved good grades in say English Literature, French and

---

[7] *Keats and Embarrassment* p.79 OUP 1974.

German in his advanced level examinations, but that now on reflection he would like to become a doctor. You would, no doubt, be flabbergasted at his change of heart and indeed, let me add, quite disenchanted if you set out to help him find a medical school which would admit him with such qualifications. For, whether we like it or not, medicine today has become almost exclusively a science-based career.

The choice of medicine as a profession may well have always been a difficult one; indeed I suppose the same is true in selecting any career, but consider this passage from Paget's delightful *Confessio Medici* published in 1908:

> Every year young men enter the medical profession who neither are born doctors nor have any great love of science, nor are helped by name or influence. Without a welcome, without money, without prospects, they fight their way into practice and in practice, they find it hard work, ill-thanked, ill-paid: there are times when they say *What call had I to be a doctor? I should have done better for myself and my wife and the children in some other calling.* But they stick to it, and that not only from necessity but from pride, honour, conviction: and Heaven, sooner or later lets them know what it thinks of them. The information comes quite as a surprise to them, being the first received from any source that they were indeed called to be doctors;

Paget also underlines the vagaries and chance involved in making up one's mind thus -

> and fathers and mothers, bent on making a doctor of one of the children, must not take the boy's mere vagaries as a sign that he is intended for that profession. *I mean to be a doctor like Father*, says he, and they rejoice over him; and a month later he wants to be a fireman or a member of Parliament. Or he is neat with his fingers, rides well, understands the ways of animals and loves to attend the minor ailments of the family: and then all that side of him goes and he gives himself to poetry or, which is worse, to music. Or he is ambitious and will make a great name, a great discovery: and again the wind catches the weathercock and he praises a leisurely life and the happiness of insignificance. His parents look in vain for such assurance as may justify action. *Time will show*, they say, and wait; but nothing happens, nothing decisive. Something must be done;

Time, still silent, is up: they determine amid hopes and fears which he hardly notices, that he shall study Medicine.

That indecision can be ended for some who are *called* and as an example, Paget quotes Lydgate's call in *Middlemarch* -

One vacation, a wet day sent him to the small home-library, to hunt once more for a book which might have some freshness for him: in vain! unless, indeed, he took down a dusty row of volumes with grey-paper backs and dingy labels - the volumes of an old Cyclopaedia which he had never disturbed .... The page he opened on was under the head of Anatomy and the first passage that drew his eyes was on the valves of the heart. He was not much acquainted with valves of any sort but he knew that *valvae* were folding doors, and through this crevice came a sudden light startling him with his first vivid notion of finely adapted mechanism in the human frame .... The moment of vocation had come and, before he got down from his chair, the world was made new to him by a presentiment of endless processes filling the vast spaces blanked out of his sight by that wordy ignorance which he had supposed to be knowledge. From that hour, Lydgate felt the growth of an intellectual passion.

Quite clearly this type of calling did not apply to Keats and medicine, nor indeed does it seem applicable to his subsequent decision to replace medicine by poetry. This later decision was a much more clear-headed, intellectual, dispassionate resolution to qualify in medicine and then to give his energy to poetry. Indeed, the objectivity of his behaviour is in strange contrast to his youthful headstrong excesses.

All of this puts into some sort of perspective the difficulties, indecisions and vagaries of change which eventually result in the production of doctors. But are we being quite fair to Keats? Was the change of emphasis such a major revolution, such a marked alteration in the direction of his life? One must remember that in his time medicine was a very different profession from what it has become today.

The care of the sick was entrusted to three groups which had evolved from quite different backgrounds - apothecaries, surgeons and physicians. The apothecaries, previously protected by the Grocers' Company, were constituted by the Royal Charter of James I in 1617. The surgeons, affiliated to the medieval guild of Barbers and Surgeons, were keen to form professional standards of their own, but it was not until 1800 that their college received the Royal Charter. The physicians on the other hand, were a small university-trained group with a Royal Charter dating back to 1518. They were the only group entitled to be called 'doctor', to charge fees, and were available for consultation by surgeons or apothecaries in difficult cases. At the beginning of the 19th century, the increase in population and demand for medical care by the common people unable to afford to pay physicians' fees led to some increase in the technical skill of apothecaries, though the College of Physicians tried to prevent them giving advice and supplying medicine to patients without the intervention of a physician. A test case which The Society of Apothecaries took to the House of Lords in 1703 produced a decision in its favour. Apothecaries were, as a result of this decision, allowed to give advice but not charge patients a fee. Many apothecaries studied surgery as well as medicine - Hammond for instance - and became members of the Surgeons' Company; these developments led in 1815 to the Apothecaries Act giving the Society legal right to grant licences to practise medicine in England and Wales.

It should be noted that Keats joined Hammond in Edmonton as an apprentice apothecary in 1810 and left him in 1815, and it was thus after his time at Guy's Hospital that he was able to sit for the recently established licentiate under the terms of the Apothecaries Act.

It is only in the last four decades that the two cultures of arts and science have become such uneasy bedfellows; the ultra-specialisation demanded of our modern medical graduates makes inevitable a separation into scientists and others - producing a 'them' and 'us' approach to life. This is altogether alien to the practice of a profession which, however deeply rooted in scientific principles is none-the-less brought to the individual patient by another individual who if not human, indeed who if not more than human, cannot be worthy of the name physician.

Undoubtedly we have pushed the pendulum too far in our obsequious admiration for science; this has produced expectations in many that if achievable at all are often bought at excessive cost and some of these expectations are in the realm of fantasy. The time is ripe for a reaction from this situation - what Isaiah Berlin calls the modern Enlightenment, in which every genuine question is supposed to have only one true answer which is true for all men, at all times and all places. Indeed medicine would be as good a starting place as any for such a reaction, for within the practice of medicine come together the twin disciplines of science and the humanities; it is the glory of the profession that the tensions produced by the expression of these disciplines are capable of such multifarious manifestations.

It could be argued that the training of a doctor is an excellent training in human behaviour, in the knowledge that is required in dealing with people, often at an emotional crisis of their lives; this may be viewed as a good starting point whatever career is eventually followed. If this is true today and I hear it on all sides, how much truer was it at the beginning of the 19th century when the split between physic and metaphysic was only starting to emerge.

We are all creatures of circumstance. Perhaps Richard Abbey and Grandmother Jennings were influenced to suggest a career in medicine to young John because of the recent administrations of Dr Hammond who attended John Jennings; were the Jennings' household not now living only a few doors along Church Street from the doctor's surgery?

Another reason why Keats may have been interested in medicine and which could have induced him to take up the profession, was the fact that he was acutely conscious of his mother's suffering and may have been irked by medical ineptitude or failure in curing her. Keats may well have felt that he could do better and set about the only way of demonstrating his ability. This may have been what he meant by his subsequent statement that he was 'ambitious of doing the world some good'.

Although Keats himself has left us no record of the reasons and difficulties surrounding his decision to become apprenticed to Hammond, it is very likely that the change was accompanied by a greater degree of disquiet and anxiety than his silence in the matter might lead one to suppose. In 1819, nine years after taking up his apprenticeship, there occurs an interesting reflection in the revised preface to *Endymion*. The preface is in the nature of an apology for what he felt were deficiencies in the work, and towards the end Keats states

> The imagination of a boy is healthy, and the mature imagination of a man is healthy; but there is a space of life between in which the soul is in a ferment, the character indecided, the way of life uncertain, the ambition thick-sighted: thence proceeds mawkishness, and all the thousand bitters ...

Is it stretching credulity too far to suggest that he was remembering his own 'indecision' and 'ferment' nine years earlier?

(ii) Apprenticeship

Thomas Hammond, apothecary, roughly comparable to a contemporary family practitioner, to whom Keats was apprenticed in mid-summer 1810[8], came from a well established medical family in Edmonton and had been trained in Guy's Hospital. He practised from No. 7 Church Street and the photograph shows the house before it was demolished in 1931; indeed the house had remained a doctor's surgery until its demolition. The picture shows a fine two-storey building set well back from the road; in the garden at one side of the house was the surgery over which it is thought that the apprentices lived. Today Church Street, Edmonton, forms part of a busy shopping centre with no trace of the 'doctor's house'. However, part of the shopping area is indeed called 'Keats's Parade' and a blue plaque, fittingly enough over an apothecary's shop, notes that this was the site of Hammond's house and mentions Keats's apprenticeship.

At the beginning of the 19th century medical training and the qualifications of those who looked after the sick, were to say the least, confused. You might consult someone who had had no training at all - merely acquired a 'reputation'; some acquired a training of sorts in the army or navy and brought their military skills into civilian practice. The Barbers' Company gave rise to the independent Company of Surgeons in 1745 which in 1800 evolved by Charter to become The Royal College of Surgeons of London. Many of these 'surgeons' at the beginning of the 19th century did not confine their practice to surgery; the concept of specialisation had hardly begun.

The legal position of the apothecaries had been established by the House of Lords' settlement in 1703 in which they might not only compound and dispense but also direct and order remedies for the treatment of disease. They were allowed to visit and prescribe but not to charge fees for this service. The latter was the province of the College of Physicians, who also granted licences to practice medicine in London but imposed conditions which made it impossible for an apothecary to compete. Indeed the difference in the results achieved by physicians and apothecaries does not seem to have been conspicuous: 'The practice of

---

[8] Most biographers give 1811 as Keats's starting date with Hammond. Gittings argues convincingly for the earlier date. - *J.K.* 1968 p.31.

Thomas Hammond's House Edmonton. It was demolished in 1931. (Photograph Fred Holland Day 1890.)

the physician does not appear to have been much superior, but it was written in infinitely more erudite and obscure language'.[9]

In 1814 in London there were thought to be 50 physicians, 70 surgeons but some 900 apothecaries and surgeon-apothecaries. As late as 1851 when medical practitioners were asked, in the Census Schedule, whether they had a medical diploma, it was found that only about one third had any qualifications.[10]

The apothecaries then occupied an important position by virtue of their numbers, training and legal position, ultimately formalised in the Act of 1815. As opposed to students of medicine at Oxford or Cambridge who acquired a great knowledge of the past writings on physic, the apothecaries were practical men[11] involved in the everyday business of caring for the sick. Their training involved the recognition of drugs and learning the complicated methods for compounding and dispensing medicines. The duties of an apprentice included accompanying his master on his rounds and perhaps taking notes when a physician was called in consultation.

He was also expected to assist at post-mortem examinations. As well as this, the trainee was no doubt involved in a number of menial tasks, sweeping and cleaning the shop, running errands and generally waiting on his master's convenience. The apprentice was therefore very much at the mercy of his master's skill and temperament. It is however, worth noting that the Society had under Bye-Law 12, a system for examining and making judgements on complaints lodged either by members or apprentices. There is no record of any complaint lodged by Keats or Hammond.

We have but one brief glimpse of Keats the apprentice in the account of a small boy at Clarke's School being dared to throw a snowball at Keats who was minding Hammond's horse in the snow.

There was plenty of spare time and on two or three afternoons a week Keats walked the two miles from the surgery to Enfield to discuss books and literary matters with his friend Cowden Clarke. Sometimes he dined with the headmaster and afterwards the two youths would talk late into the night, after which Keats returned to Edmonton. He continued his

---

[9] Wall, Cameron and Underwood (W.C.U.). *A History of the Worsh. Soc. Apoth. I*, OUP 1963 p.77.
[10] (W.C.U.) I. p.190.
[11] Before 1800 only one woman applied for Freedom of the Soc. In 1727 a Mrs Read applied but was refused, not on the grounds of her sex but because she was not qualified to pass an examination - W.C.U. I, p.84.

translation of the *Aeneid* which had been started during the latter part of his time at school. There is no doubt that this was a pleasant time for Keats, devoted more to literature than to medicine. Cowden Clarke sums it up by saying that 'it was the most placid period of his painful life'.

It is an extraordinary fact that this five-year period of Keats's apprenticeship with Hammond is, with one minor exception, totally devoid of documentation. The young poet who was to give us such remarkable letters at a later phase of his life tells us nothing of his daily round with Hammond. The exception referred to occurs as a passage in a long letter to George Keats written over a number of days in September 1819. Keats writes: Tuesday -

> You see I keep adding a sheet daily till I send the packet off - which I shall not do for a few days as I am inclined to write a good deal: for there can be nothing so rembrancing and enchaining as a good long letter be it composed of what it may - From the time you left me, our friends say I have altered completely - am not the same person - perhaps in this letter I am for in a letter one takes up one's existence from the time we last met - I dare say you have altered also - every man does - Our bodies every seven years are completely fresh - materiald - seven years ago it was not this hand that clench'd itself against Hammond - ...

This remark about Hammond, principally on the evidence of George Keats, is always taken as indicating that there had been a quarrel of some sort between apprentice and master.

Attempting to substantiate some details of his apprenticeship, we find that many of Keats's biographers imply or state that there was with Keats a second apprentice who is credited with the remark that Keats was 'an idle loafing fellow, always writing poetry'. The first mention of this second apprentice is in Sir Sidney Colvin's *John Keats* published in 1917. Now Colvin had already published a smaller biography of Keats that went through a large number of editions - or rather reprints - the last of which appeared in 1906 in which there is no mention of a 'second apprentice'. But in the later and more complete work we find the reference to 'an idle loafing fellow' given in quotation marks indicating that Colvin was quoting an individual or a document. Unfortunately he does not give documentary support for his statement. It is surprising and disappointing that Colvin - a careful archivist - gives no clarification on this point, and examination of his available correspondence in Keats

House, Hampstead, the British Library and at the Fitzwilliam Museum, Cambridge where Colvin was curator from 1873-85, provides no clue as to the origin of the quotation or the reason for its insertion in Colvin's second biography of Keats.

It is of interest to note that the Regulations of the Society of Apothecaries (Bye-Law 8)[12] state that - No-one must have more than one apprentice until he has kept shop for three years, later increased to five years, and thereby proved his capacity as a trainer of youth. After that time a member might have two apprentices, and during the year before the expiration of the term of the elder apprentice a third might be added.

Thus, if in fact Hammond did have two apprentices it throws more light on Hammond's standing as a trainer than on Keats's attitude to his work.

Keats spent the period 1810 to 1815 as Hammond's apprentice and we have his signature for his entry to Guy's Hospital in October 1815. The Counting House Record at Guy's gives details of the names of the apprentice and his sponsor as well as the location of practice of the sponsor and dates. Examination of the Counting House records does not show any other apprentice sponsored by Hammond who could have been in Edmonton during the time of Keats's apprenticeship. We find a number of entries in the record book for the period 1778-1813 emphasising the Hammond family's medical training. Thus William Hammond signed on for six months on June 18th 1807 being apprenticed to William Hammond - presumably his father - of South Gate; likewise William Hammond is entered for February 9th 1780 and Thomas Hammond - Keats's master - joined on October 2nd 1786. However, the record does not show any other apprentice sponsored by Hammond who could have been in Edmonton for the period 1810-15, that is during Keats's apprenticeship.

There is however, record of another apprentice named John Fothergill, sponsored by Mr Maule of Edmonton, who signed on for one year on October 4th 1813. Assuming that Fothergill's apprenticeship with Maule had lasted the usual four or five years, Fothergill would have been active in Edmonton during the period 1809-13, thus possibly coinciding with part of Keats's period with Hammond. Fothergill would have been Keats's senior by about two years and might well have resented the literary inclinations of a junior colleague. Unfortunately we know nothing either

---

[12] W.C.U. I, p.1617-1815.

of Fothergill or Maule to substantiate the possibilities that the former was in fact the second apprentice referred to in Colvin's later biography of Keats. An outside possibility is that the second apprentice trained at another medical school - the most likely being St. Bartholomew's. As records of students attending that hospital do not begin until 1842, there is no way of discovering if the second apprentice could have been a Bart's man.

(iii) Medical School

It is perhaps misleading to use the term medical school to describe the institution to which Keats presented himself for hospital training in October 1815. But it was none-the-less probably closer to our present day understanding of the complex of laboratories, lecture theatres, demonstration rooms and hospital buildings of a modern medical school, than many other institutions offering medical training in the country at that time. Indeed, Guy's at the time of the Apothecaries Act of 1815 was the only institution capable of providing all the medical teaching required by the Society for its Diploma. The United Hospitals comprised St. Thomas's Hospital and Guy's Hospital; they had been brought together for the purposes of teaching in 1768. Situated just over London Bridge in the Borough of Southwark, St. Thomas's had in 1814 added a new wing containing an anatomy museum, a dissecting room and a lecture theatre. By tradition, anatomy including dissection, together with lectures in surgery, took place at St. Thomas's while medical subjects including chemistry and materia medica were given at Guy's. In this way the teaching resources of both hospitals in terms of patients, attending staff and buildings, combined to provide what seems to have been excellent clinical training on a co-operative basis that has not been bettered in modern times. Indeed one does not have to be a cynic to postulate that there may have been a good deal more acrimony among the 'United' hospitals if contemporary experience as expressed by Todd 'twinning' or Lord Flower's rationalisation of medical education in London, is anything to go by.

Medicine in the early 19th century was very different from the science-based technically advanced subject we know today. Laennec's discovery of the stethoscope was not reported until 1819 and the great

Guy's Hospital. North Front of Guy's. Engraving by J. Pass c.1800.

pioneers Pasteur and Koch, the founders of the modern science of bacteriology, did not have an impact until the century was well advanced.

In Keats's day the physician had few diagnostic aids; the use of the clinical thermometer was not a routine until the mid 19th century, and it is doubtful if Keats was examined with the aid of a stethoscope, but it is probable that Dr Clark used one in Rome.

Perhaps the biggest change in clinical medicine which occurred during the first half of the 19th century was an alteration in emphasis away from *symptoms* and towards recognising the importance of *signs*. Thus the patient's history of symptoms could be correlated with the doctor's findings, i.e. signs, which he elicited on examining the patient. There is for example, no record of any physical examination having been carried out at Guy's in the year 1823[13] - two years after Keats's death. Today medical students are taught the clinical importance of both the patient's history and physical examination. In teaching the latter we emphasise the apparently logical steps in examination, namely inspection, palpation, percussion and auscultation. The latter followed the use of Laennec's stethoscope and in fact became a routine method before the other techniques in physical examination became a matter of standard practice. Treatment was largely confined to resting the patient or ordering diets of one sort or another; few drugs had real benefit and some treatments such as bleeding, which was widely practised, did far more harm than good. Surgery, without anaesthetics, was an awesome and terrifying ordeal for patient, operator and onlooker.

Keats joined the United Hospitals in October 1815; having paid his office fee of £1.2s. on October 1st, he paid the further fee of £25.4s. the following day to sign on as a surgical pupil for twelve months. He obtained a set of medical instruments, a supply of notebooks for 2s.2d. and standard medical texts. Armed with the *London Dissector* he set forth like any other medical student on the awe-inspiring voyage of practical medical training epitomised by the dissecting room. And we have a good account of what dissecting room conditions at this period were like from the description of John Flint South - a student at St. Thomas's two years before Keats arrived.

> The dissecting room in 1813 was a squarish room above the eastern half of the laboratory lighted by two windows eastward

---

[13] Newman, C. *The Evolution of Medical Education in the Nineteenth Century*, OUP 1957.

and a square lantern in the ceiling .... A large fireplace and copper, used to prepare the subjects for dissection, was at the south side and a large leaden sink under the windows was indiscriminately used for washing hands and washing subjects and discharging all the filth. In this room were usually standing about a dozen tables with their corresponding bundles, and six to eight pupils to each, so that on average the room was crammed with seventy to eighty people, clad in filthy linen or stuff dissecting gowns, so that there was scarce possibility of moving.

The supply of bodies for dissection was provided by 'body snatchers' or 'resurrection' men as they were called. The principal source of supply was the London graveyards where the sextons were usually in the pay of the resurrection men. The trade was carried on discreetly, the bodies being removed at night to avoid detection. This practice of procuring subjects for anatomy departments was regulated by teachers from various anatomy schools who had formed the Anatomy Club so that among other things the price paid to the resurrection men could be regulated. Four guineas was the usual price paid per subject. This unofficial but condoned system of obtaining bodies for dissection prevailed until the scandal of the Burke and Hare murders in Edinburgh led to the Anatomy Act of 1832.

Keats lived with his student companions in lodgings near the hospitals which he attended daily - dissection, anatomy and surgery at St. Thomas's and medical subjects at Guy's. Keats signed on for two terms' lectures in anatomy and physiology, two courses in the theory and practice of medicine, two in chemistry and one term's course in materia medica. These courses when successfully completed would allow Keats to attain the recently introduced Licentiate of the Society of Apothecaries, fitting him to be what we would now call a general practitioner. But the strong surgical bias in his courses suggests (at any rate) that at this early stage of hospital training, Keats may have had ambitions of obtaining the Membership of the Royal College of Surgeons.

Keats was very lucky in his personal encounters in his early days at Guy's. The senior lecturer in anatomy - Astley Cooper - one of the masters of English surgery - put Keats under the care of his own dresser George Cooper. Cooper and his friend Frederick Tyrrell, took Keats into their lodging and they all shared a common sitting room. Cooper later had a successful general practice at Brentford, while Tyrrell had already had surgical experience at the Battle of Waterloo.

Frequent visits from his brothers Tom and George added to the gaiety of this student group. A family friend, also a medical student, was Henry Newmarch who seems to have pulled Keats's leg about his poetry, often provoking retaliation from the admiring brothers. Another new friend at this stage was Joseph Severn, finishing his apprenticeship as an engraver and painting in his spare time.

When the more senior students Cooper and Tyrrell moved on to other courses, Keats was left alone and to save expense moved in with two other students, George Wilson MacKereth and Henry Stephens. Stephens, who had literary aspirations, is remembered for he later patented the well-known ink called after its inventor. To Stephens we are indebted for the oft quoted 'thing of beauty' anecdote delightfully recorded by Sir Benjamin Ward Richardson:

> In a room, Mr Stephens told me, he was always at the window, peering into space, so that the window-seat was spoken of by his comrades as 'Keats's place'. Here his inspiration seemed to come most freely. Here, one evening in the twilight, the two students sitting together, Stephens at his medical studies, Keats at his dreaming, Keats breaks out to Stephens that he has composed a new line:
> "A thing of beauty is a constant joy"
> "What think you of that, Stephens?"
> "It has the true ring, but is wanting in some way" replies the latter, as he dips once more into his medical studies.
> An interval of silence, and again the poet: "A thing of beauty is a joy for ever". "What do you think of that, Stephens?"
> "That it will live for ever."

The impression one gains of medical student John Keats is of an attractive, vivacious personality and an appearance that led one of his early minor poet friends, Felton Mathew, to comment that 'a painter or sculptor might have taken him for a study of the Greek masters ...! His eye was more critical than tender, and so was his mind'.[14] It was during this period at Guy's that he acquired the nickname 'Junkets'. We have brief sketches of him taking lecture notes, occasionally drawing flowers in the margins or letting his mind wander on a sunbeam to Oberon and

---

[14] KC, II, 185.

fairyland. All of this is quite understandable, particularly perhaps to medical students who may have had to sit through interminable lectures dealing with the minutiae of the inguinal canal or the relations of the femoral artery.

He kept up his friendship with Cowden Clarke to whom he would give accounts of his lectures or of bear-baiting sessions he had attended in the Borough of Southwark. Through Clarke he met Leigh Hunt; Keats walked out to Hunt's cottage in the Vale of Health carrying a sheaf of poems with him. Hunt records -

> the impression made upon me by the exuberant specimen of genuine though young poetry that were laid before me, and the promise which was seconded by the fine, fervid countenance of the writer. We became intimate on the spot, and I found the young Poet's heart as warm as his imagination.

During the later period of his time at Guy's Hospital Keats seems to have developed reservations about the practice of surgery. There is quite an important distinction to be made between Keats the physician and Keats the surgeon. He had the ability, the training and possibly the motivation to be a physician but surgery was a different matter. He had been a dresser to William Lucas, son of Hammond's superb teacher, but unfortunately Lucas Jr. did not possess his father's skill. He was regarded as no more than a butcher, leading Astley Cooper to comment 'making us all shudder from the apprehension of his opening up arteries or committing some other error'. John Flint South describes the scene in the operating theatre at this period:-

> ... I began to attend the operations in the hospital theatre; this was for some time a very hard trial for me. I was always very anxious to see all I could and soon got over the blood-shedding which necessarily ensued; and so long as the patient did not make much noise I got on very well, but if the cries were great, and specially if they came from a child, I was quickly upset, had to leave the theatre, and not infrequently fainted; but generally on recovering, if the operations were continuing, returned to my place to see the end. The heat had probably something to do with this failing, for the theatre was almost invariably crammed to excess, and the atmosphere almost stifling ...

Keats in operating theatre: Imaginary drawing of Keats by R.M. Wingert, 1908 who was also a student at Guy's.

In this atmosphere, more reminiscent of a torture chamber than an operating theatre, the one really civilised influence came from the surgeon, Astley Cooper. Even today surgeons often have a reputation for brash pragmatism engendered in an 'open and find out' approach to problems which is looked at rather disdainfully by their more contemplative physician colleagues. However, when the technical and manipulative skills of the craftsman surgeon come together in one person with the integrative constructive power of a physician, the result is usually an extraordinary being and occasionally a great man. And this is what Astley Cooper was. He was not only a superb technical surgeon but he was a humane and interesting personality as well. He took a keen interest in his pupils and gave them the best of his clinical teaching as well as the benefit of his wide and extended personal experience. His lectures were enlivened by anecdotes in one of which he displays a fine surgical scepticism of physicians:

'In disease medical men guess; if they cannot ascertan a disease, they call it nervous'. How little things change.

Astley Cooper (1768-1841). From a painting by Charles Penny, engraved in 1829 by J.H. Robinson.

Astley Cooper who was one of the great founders of modern surgical technique, epitomised the attributes required of a surgeon in his phrase 'an eagle's eye, a lady's hand, and a lion's heart'. He could be moved by a patient's plight; Flint South records the case of a child who was taken to Cooper to have a naevus (a birthmark) removed. Whether, on seeing the child Cooper was immediately aware of the pain the operation would cause, or perhaps that the prognosis was hopeless, or for whatever reason, Flint writes: 'I do not know whether it was a lovely child or not, but when brought into the room it smiled very sweetly upon him, and Cooper burst into tears'.

In his lectures Cooper warned his students not to become surgeons unless they had the temperament for it and quoted the Guy's dresser who accidentally opened an artery. It is impossible not to believe that Astley Cooper had a major influence on Keats. From him he may have had insight into the troubled decisions awkward compromises and fine judgements demanded by a discipline which all too often may not necessarily be to the patient's benefit. The warning given in Cooper's lectures may well be the origin of Keats's later remark 'I have forgotten all surgery'. Describing a minor surgical operation which he had performed, Keats gives his verdict on surgery to his friend Brown thus:

Charcoal drawing of Keats in 1817, by his friend Joseph Severn.

It was my last, and it consisted in opening a man's temporal artery. I did it with the utmost nicety, but reflecting on what passed in my mind at the time, my dexterity seemed a miracle - I never took up the lancet again.

Keats had rejected surgery and while he does not exactly present himself as an enthusiastic physician at any time, he returned to the idea of practising *medicine* on a number of occasions suggesting that his medical training was never too far below the surface of his thinking.

In July 1816 Keats presented himself for the Licentiate of the Society of Apothecaries. In order to sit for the examination he produced a testimonial from Hammond, suggesting that if there had been a disagreement between them, Hammond did not consider it too serious, and evidence of courses studied in anatomy, physiology, chemistry and materia medica. The scrutiny of qualifications for sitting the examination which one must remember was the first after the new Apothecaries Act, was quite stringent, and the failure rate in the examination itself quite high - two of Keats's contemporaries failed but Keats satisfied his examiners. There is therefore no reason to believe that Keats was not properly trained and suitably qualified to become a practitioner; in the

Thomas Wakeley (1795-1862). Founder-editor of *The Lancet;* a fellow student at Guy's 1815. Portrait painted 1840. Glass negative of portrait by J.K. Meadows (1790-1874) engraved by William Henry Egleton (fl. 1830-1870)

event, he chose never to practise formally but the experience of his training and his hospital life have left certain influences which I will deal with later.

In May 1818, almost two years after qualifying, and declaring his preference for poetry rather than medicine, he records his decision as regards medicine quite objectively in his letter to Reynolds written from Teignmouth:-

> Were I to study physic or rather medicine again, - I feel it would not make the least difference to my poetry; when the mind is in its infancy a Bias is in reality a Bias, but when we have acquired more strength, a Bias becomes no Bias. Every department of knowledge we see excellent and calculated towards a great whole. I am so convinced of this that I am glad at not having given away my medical books, which I shall again look over to keep alive the little I know thitherwards ...

CHAPTER IV

Medicine and Literature

There has always been a close relation between medicine and literature. We might I suppose, begin with Luke - the Beloved physician who certainly left his mark on literature; even earlier, Hippocrates - the founder of modern medicine might be mentioned or even Aesculapius himself - the Greek god of medicine who - mentioned by Homer - may actually have existed as a person. He however, had little time for writing, being fully occupied with casting out Devils, at which he became so adept that he annoyed Zeus who then finished him off with a thunderbolt.

Other notable author-physicians have included Rabelais and Thomas Browne of *Religio Medici* fame, Tobias Smollett and George Crabbe. The latter provided a description of the workhouse apothecary in *The Village*, written in 1783, which must have included an experience not so very different from that of Keats in Edmonton. Goethe, Sainte-Beuve and Blackmore must be included in this list; Oliver Wendell Holmes and Weir Mitchell are two representatives from the United States. More recently there is Gogarty, Conan Doyle and Somerset Maugham. Chekhov is a very interesting example, for although he initially trained as a doctor, his main occupation was clearly literature, but medicine claimed his interest from time to time so that at odd intervals we find him actually looking after patients. Many of these doctors who made a name in literature lived at a time when medicine or physic was part of any gentleman's education; modern specialisation has put an end to all that. One more example must be quoted, namely Robert Bridges. Bridges was a physician, a Fellow of the Royal College of Physicians, who in the latter part of his life devoted his time entirely to literature - eventually becoming Poet Laureate. Among his works is a treatise on Beauty showing Keatsean influences. Indeed Bridges in his *A Critical Introduction to Keats* gives a superb summary of Keats's position in English literature in the form of an accolade which is probably still true today:

> If one English poet might be recalled today from the dead to continue the work which he left unfinished on earth, it is probable that the crown of his country's desire would be set on the head of John Keats, for he was smitten down in his youth in the very maturing of powers which, having already produced work of the utmost unrivalled beauty, held a promise of incredible things.

But now a question has to be asked: allowing for the few direct references to medicine made by Keats in his letters, if you had not been aware of his medical training, would you from reading his poetry suspect that he had been a doctor? In fact, does medicine show through in his poems?

Many have found little if any, evidence of medicine in his work. For instance, Phyllis G. Mann complains that -

> It is vain to search Keats's correspondence for direct information about his life as a surgeon's apprentice and a medical student ....[15]

This refers to Keats's early life and relates to correspondence not to poetry, but a much more general view is put by F.M. Owen which I have already mentioned in Chapter I.

> For five years Keats prepared himself for the medical profession. It is strange how little trace we find of this work in his poems. It would seem as if he had been living a double life at the time and that while he walked the hospitals his mind was straying in the old classic fields or in the 'realms of gold' of Spenser's fairy world; for neither science nor the mechanism of the body, nor the subtle connection of the body and mind ever seem to have specially touched his imagination.[16]

This is a conclusion with which I have no sympathy, for while Owen's premise may well be correct in that Keats was probably living his life at two levels, he was only too well aware of the interaction of mind and body not to mention the clear influences of his medical training on his

---

[15] *K-S.M.B.* No. 12. 1961 p.21.
[16] Owen, F.M. *J.K.* Kegan Paul. 1880 p5.

technique of observation and even on his very choice of word and phrase. We do not have to look very far for the 'subtle connection of the body and mind'; consider *Ode to a Nightingale* -

> The weariness, the fever, and the fret
> Here, where men sit and hear each other groan;
> Where palsy shakes a few, sad, last gray hairs,
> Where youth grows pale, and spectre-thin and dies;
> Where but to think is to be full of sorrow
> And leaden-eyed despairs,
> Where Beauty cannot keep her lustrous eyes
> On new Love pine at them beyond to-morrow.

This is surely a vision of the world as seen by a man who had experienced the way in which illness changes life, and not only an almost certain reference to brother Tom's tuberculosis. The couplet -

> Here where men sit and hear each other groan;
> Where palsy shakes a few, sad, last gray hairs

brings to mind a waiting-room full of patients such as Keats must have experienced when he was a dresser at Guy's: the image is indeed not all that far removed from a large out-patient clinic in a modern department of, say, neurology.

There are a number of occasions in the poems when Keats mentions blood in a graphic, unexpected, incongruous and what I can only call a 'medical' way. For instance, towards the end of *Endymion* in Book IV he describes the Indian maiden:

> My Indian bliss!
> My river-lilly bud! One human kiss!
> Warm as a dove's nest among summer trees
> And warm with dew at ooze from living blood.

We find the phrase '... his ears gush'd blood' in *Isabella*. Or again, in *Otho the Great* Keats talks of blood in a much more dynamic cardiovascular sense:

> A young man's heart, by Heaven's blessing, is
> A wide world, where a thousand new-borne hopes

> Empurple fresh the melancholy blood:
> But an old Man's is narrow, tenantless
> Of hopes and stuffed with many memories
> Which, being pleasant, ease the heavy pulse -
> Painfull, clog up and stagnate.

In *Ode to Fanny* we again find Keats using the term 'blood' in a medical context, in that bleeding was supposed to improve or ease the patient:

> Physician Nature! let my spirit blood;
> Oh, ease my heart of verse and let me rest;
> Throw me upon thy tripod till the flood
> Of stifling members ebbs from my full breast.

E.W. Goodall[17] in his interesting paper drew attention to these and other references to passages in Keats's poems which indicate a medical training. Thus at the very end of *The Eve of St. Agnes* when Keats is summing up his characters and telling us what happened to each of them, we have what amounts to a little clinical cameo on the fate of Angela, the old woman -

> Angela the old
> Died palsy-twitch'd, with meagre face deform

In *The Cap and Bells*, an unfinished fairy tale of comic irony that contains veiled references to some contemporary literary figures and perhaps to the royal scandal in which the Regent threatened to bring Princess Caroline to trial for adultery, we find in stanza LXX -

> "The Emperor's horrid bad; yes, that's my cue"
> Some histories say that this was Hum's last speech
> That, being fuddled, he went reeling through
> The corridor, and scarce upright could reach
> The stair-head; that being glutted as a leech
> And us'd, as we ourselves have just now said
> To manage stairs reversely, like a peach

---

[17] *Guy's Hosp. Gazette*, June 1936.

> Too ripe, he fell, being puzzled in the head
> With liquor and the staircase: verdict -
> *found stone dead.*

Succinct enough for a case report in *The Lancet*.

And then in one of his earliest poems beginning 'I stood tip-toe upon a little hill' in which according to Leigh Hunt 'he stood beside the gate that leads from the Battery on Hampstead Heath into a field by Caen Wood' (which is of course Ken Wood), Keats describes the Heath in June:

> The breezes were ethereal and pure
> And crept through half-closed lattices to cure
> The languid sick; it cool'd their fever'd sleep,
> And soothed them into slumbers full and deep.
> Soon they awake clear eyed: nor burnt with thirsting,
> Nor with hot fingers, nor with temples bursting:
> And springing up, they met the wond'ring sight
> Of their dear friends, nigh foolish with delight;
> Who feel their arms, and breasts and kiss and stare,
> And on their placid foreheads part the hair.

The direct references in the poems to medical matters are therefore few, but Goellnicht (see Chapter I, p.18) has provided a whole range of new insights and should be consulted in detail.

Before leaving the poems there is one other possible medical influence on Keats's language which I would like to suggest. Astley Cooper, whose lectures Keats attended, gives a case report,

> I shall have occasion to mention to you a most extraordinary case, in which the functions of the mind were suspended from an interruption of the circulation in the brain, for upwards of thirteen months; the patient having as it were, drunk the cup of Lethe during all that period [Lethe was one of the rivers of Hades - drinking its waters produced oblivion] from that moment ... his mind had remained in a state of perfect oblivion. He had drunk as it were the cup of Lethe, he had suffered a complete death, as far as regarded his mental, and almost all his bodily powers.

The similarity to the opening lines of the *Ode to a Nightingale*, is striking, in which Astley Cooper's medical speculation is transmuted by Keats's poetic imagination to,

> My heart aches, and a drowsy numbness pains
> My sense, as though of hemlock I had drunk,
> Or emptied some dull opiate to the drains
> One minute past, and Lethe-wards had sunk:

In his letters Keats refers to medicine, usually in terms of falling back on the profession if things did not go well with him, but he also had something to say in favour of his choice of poetry. In May 1819 writing to the George Keatses he says -

> I have been at different times turning it in my head whether I should go to Edinburgh and study for a physician; I am afraid I should not take kindly to it, I am sure I could not take fees and yet I should like to do so; it is not worse than writing poems and hanging them up, to be flyblown on the Reviewshambles ...

This is the only record we have of his wish to specialise as a physician; quite clearly medicine is only his second choice. In two letters, one at the end of May, the other on June 9th 1819 written to Sarah Jeffery, Keats toys with the idea of being a ship's doctor:

> ... I have the choice as it were of two Poisons (yet I ought not to call this a Poison) - the one is voyaging to and from India for a few years; the other is leading a fevrous life alone with Poetry - This latter will suit me best - for I cannot resolve to give up by Studies ...

and

> Your advice about the Indiaman is a very wise advice because it just suits me, though you are a little in the wrong concerning its destroying the energies of Mind; on the contrary it would be the finest thing in the world to strengthen them.

There then follows a tirade against the bad treatment of poets by the English at the end of which he again comes back to the Indiaman:-

> For all this I will not go on board an Indiaman, nor for examples

sake run my head into dark alleys: I dare say my discipline is to come, and plenty of it too ...

Thus again, despite his ambivalence, the medical option takes second place.

From the Isle of Wight in July 1819, writing to Fanny Keats, he again demonstrates the way in which medicine was to be his second choice in case his 'pen' failed. It is his most explicit statement on the subject:

> I think I told you the purpose for which I retired to this place - to try the fortune of my Pen once more, and indeed I have some confidence in my success: but in every event, believe me my dear sister, I shall be sufficiently comfortable as, if I cannot lead that life of competence and society I should wish, I have enough knowledge of my gallipots to ensure me an employment and maintainance.

Even as late as June 1820 the same theme recurs in his letter to Brown:

> My book is coming out with very low hopes, though not spirits on my part. That shall be my last trial; not succeeding, I shall try what I can do in the Apothecary line.

In a long letter to Reynolds from Teignmouth on May 3rd, 1818, there appears not only the famous passage

> Were I to study physic or rather Medicine again ...

but also two other reflections by Keats which to my mind show strong elements of a medical background. Thus,

> You are sensible no man can set down Venery as a bestial or joyless thing until he is sick of it and therefore all philosophizing on it would be mere wording. Until we are sick we understand not; - in fine, as Byron says "Knowledge is Sorrow".

Here Keats sets out to explain that only experience of a subject gives one a right to an understanding that gives our opinions validity, and then he seems to be struck by the word 'sick' which in the first instance he uses in the sense of too much; and then quickly he uses the term for a second time but now sick is used to mean illness. In explaining that understanding requires experience, he chooses a medical context for his example.

Towards the end of this long letter Keats puts down what he calls -

> a simile of human life as far as I now perceive it ... - Well - I compare human life to a large Mansion of Many Apartments, two of which I can only describe, the doors of the rest being as yet shut upon me - The first we step into we call the infant or thoughtless Chamber, in which we remain as long as we do not think - We remain there a long while, and notwithstanding the doors of the second Chamber remain wide open, showing a bright appearance, we care not to hasten to it; but are at length imperceptibly impelled by the awakening of the thinking principle - within us - we no sooner get into the second Chamber which I shall call the Chamber of Maiden-Thought, than we become intoxicated with the light and the atmosphere, we see nothing but pleasant wonders, and think of delaying there for ever in delight: However among the effects this breathing is father of is that tremendous one of sharpening one's vision into the heart and nature of Man - of convincing ones nerves that the World is full of Misery and Heartbreak, Pain, Sickness and oppression - whereby This Chamber of Maiden Thought becomes gradually darken'd and at the same time on all sides of it many doors are set open - but all dark - all leading to dark passages ...

This view of the world shows a progression from innocent thoughtlessness to the ultimate realisation of the wickedness of the world - a realisation that is brought about by our experience in the world - at least some of which is caused by our understanding of 'Misery', 'Heartbreak', 'Pain' and 'Sickness'.

A very nice example of the way in which Keats's thinking was entirely modern in regard to the mental origins of physical disease, quite in line with contemporary psychosomatic views, is given in his letter to John Taylor in September 1819.

> And if this sort of atmosphere is a mitigation to the energies of a strong man; how much more must it injure a weak one - unoccupied - unexercised - For what is the cause of so many men maintaining a good state in Cities but occupation - An idle man; a man who is not sensitively alive to self interest in a city cannot continue long

in good Health - This is easily explained. If you were to walk leisurely through an unwholesome path in the fens, with a little horror of them, you would be sure to have your ague. But let macbeth cross the same path, with the dagger in the air leading him on, and he would never have an ague or anything like it. You should give these things a serious consideration.

Writing to the George Keatses on Brown's ponderous method of composition, he has a little joke with a medical flavour:

Brown has been walking up and down the room a breeding - now at this moment he is being delivered of a couplet - and I dare say will be as well as can be expected - Gracious - he has twins!

These examples from the letters indicate that, even if Keats consciously rejected medicine in favour of poetry, subconsciously, perhaps even against his will, the ideas and imagery of his training came to the surface in his writing. Reynolds said that Keats never spoke of his student days except to regret that he had endured 'a one of them'. This might be taken as his conscious rejection of the profession but when faced with an acute medical problem the situation could be different. There is the anecdote, quoted in Dorothy Hewlett's *Life of Keats*, that one of his friends (Wells or Horne) related that some time after Keats had given up medicine, they were walking together when Keats rushed forward to the help of a poor man who had met with an accident. His leg was broken and Keats immediately set it in a 'masterly manner'. As they walked away Keats said that 'there was great pleasure in alleviating suffering; but it was a dreadful profession on account of having to witness so much'.

Admittedly one has to search carefully and look long for these overt or covert references to medicine in Keats's writing. Rather than tracing direct medical references, Stuart Sperry considers the subtle manner in which Keats's scientific training induced a way of thinking and a use of words. Sperry points out the way in which his study of chemistry influenced Keats's ideas on poetic composition. One of Keats's lecturers in chemistry, William Babington, defined his subject as - 'The science of Composition and Decomposition, of the heterogeneous particles of matter'. In a letter to Haydon we find Keats using very similar terminology to describe his perception of Beauty:

innumerable composition and decomposition which takes place

between the intellect and its thousand materials before it arrives at
that trembling, delicate and snail-horn perception of Beauty:

the analogy is clear that the words used to describe a chemical reaction can also be used to explain the origin of the perception of Beauty. Indeed Sperry writes of this under the title of 'the chemistry of the poetic process'.

Sperry also comments on the manner in which *sensation* is central to Keats's understanding of the process of poetic composition -

Poetry for Keats finds origin in what he means by sensation. At the same time poetry exists to express and to communicate *sensation*.

Now Keats only defined sensation once and that was in his lecture notes taken at Guy's:

Sensation is an impression made on the extremities of the Nerves conveyed to the Brain. Volition is the contrary of sensation - it proceeds from the internal to the external parts.

An example of how Keats used the term *sensation* in this context is to be found in his letter to Bailey in November 1817, in the famous passage in which he speaks of 'the holiness of the Hearts affections'. Later he writes ...

I have never yet been able to perceive how anything can be known for truth by consequitive reasoning - and yet it must be - can it be that even the greatest Philosopher ever arrived at his goal without putting numerous objections - However it may be, O, for a Life of Sensations rather than of thoughts.

Here Keats puts forward the view that the source of creative inspiration is a careful examination of external objects and analysis of the sensations which they arouse. This would not seem to be too far removed from the objectives of any scientific method and of medicine in particular.

At this stage it seems necessary to look at medicine and literature for points of similarity and differences; are they merely two expressions of the same life-force, two facets of the same driving spirit?

Medicine quite clearly is at one level a practical pragmatic profession. It has fairly clear-cut if very difficult aims to relieve the sick and if possible to cure and prevent illness. The profession has in most countries an administration to maintain standards of practice and to enforce certain codes of behaviour. Those who practise in this way give rise to the well-known image of 'the doctor' in the community or hospital and for which work they receive payment. Medicine is therefore a job - at its lowest. But what of medicine at its highest; can we separate any form of medical ethic from the mundane process of earning one's daily bread? It is certainly my view that such a medical ethic exists; by its nature it is secretive and not easily perceived and is open to any number of misinterpretations. Thus it differs from literature which in a major respect only comes into existence after it has been made public. The medical ethic which I contemplate consists of one major and two lesser, though very important parts. The major part is service and the other two, teaching and research. By service I mean only service to the patient by the doctor. This is the paramount attribute of medical ethic. Service to the patient may be carried out on behalf of the doctor by any number of other agencies including *par excellence*, the nursing profession. Without these agencies there remains only the doctor confronted with his patient to provide the purest form of service. In contemporary medicine many difficulties arise in pursuing this form of practice not the least of which is a whole army of paramedical services often well intentioned but not always enlightened, which may intervene between doctor and patient. For the doctor himself, the major problem remains as it has always been, the humane personal application of the fruits of scientific discovery to the individual patient. Experience shows that medicine practised in this way comes to dominate one's life to such a degree that many other aspects are excluded; medicine therefore can even become a way of knowledge and a way of life.

By literature we mean the pursuit of the profession of writing, profession being used in a much more ill-defined and less formal way than when applied to medicine. At its purest the pursuit of literature is epitomised by the poet. In his examination of this subject entitled *A Prologue to Keats*, Middleton Murry explains what he means by true literature:

> True literature is everything or nothing. It is either the vehicle of a final human truth or it is as important as the taste of caviare and essentially of the same nature as the taste of caviare. There is no comfortable compromise between these positions ...

> I do not say that literature has always occupied or will always occupy this supreme position. Neither I, nor any man, can know truly what has been in the past or may be in the future. But in the age in which we live true literature is of a more vital importance than either Religion or Science. For Religion has lost contact with the living reality from which alone derives validity and truth; and Science in its eagerness to know the external world has forgotten to explore the instrument of knowledge - man himself.
>
> The science of man ... is fallen into the hands of people like the psychoanalysts who, whatever their sincerity and seriousness, are mere children by the side of a true literary creator.

Writing in 1924 Murry clearly had some reservations about the direction science was taking, but his comments on literature in general and Keats in particular are worth quoting in full:

> It seemed to me that by using the letters of Keats as a key to his poems I might be able to reveal the nature of the pure poet and to show how utterly different from the process of ordinary understanding is the process of a pure poet's knowledge and how infinitely superior as a means to apprehending the truth; to show how close yet how strange is the relation between such a poet's life-experience and his poetic expression ... I have found it impossible to speak directly of that identity between Beauty and Truth which I have come to know, in my going on to tell the history of the poet who proclaimed this same identity one hundred years ago -
>
> > Beauty is Truth, Truth Beauty - *that is all*
> > *Ye know on earth and all ye need to know*
>
> I do not think it is presumption on my part to declare that these lines have never been understood; at least I have never seen any evidence that they have been understood, just as I have seen no evidence that Keats himself had been understood. If he had been understood, the history of English literature during the nineteenth century would have been different from what it was and perhaps many things besides literature would have been different. For literature is not a pastime; it is a vehicle of unutterable truth.

Thus both medicine and literature in the higher reaches of their practice, have great similarity in that they become a way of knowledge or truth for that body of men who practise their separate professions in their unique and personal ways.

Whatever may be said for or against this proposition, it has always seemed clear to me that the spring which drives men to different endeavours, whether they be scientific or literary or indeed of any other nature, is wound by the same central Life-Force - God if you like - the common energy source - the unleashing of which is just as likely to produce a new poem or picture, a symphony or a new scientific fact.

CHAPTER V

Keats and Tuberculosis

If Keats returned today, he might well be impressed with some of the changes and inventions of the modern world, radio, television, space technology, the Channel Tunnel; he would certainly be impressed by the advances in medicine, and particularly in treatment, such as the modern chemotherapy of tuberculosis, the disease which killed him. It is of some interest that, in his bicentenary year, tuberculosis, in a number of countries is still causing problems by an increase in incidence and, the evolution of antibiotic-resistant bacilli, against a background of deprivation in some sections of the community, and the modern plague of AIDS.

In his day nothing was known of its cause, for the microbe responsible for his disease was not described until 1882 by Robert Koch. The nature of the condition which killed so many remained a mystery; some may have thought it 'catching' or infectious, and the attitude of the police in Rome by scraping walls and burning furniture after Keats's death is a good example of official concern with the possibility of contagion, but there was no way of knowing the true nature of the communicability of tuberculosis until Koch's discovery of the microbe and the method of passing it on from one individual to another by 'droplet spread' had been elucidated. Tuberculosis may of course affect any part of the body, and in severe infections more than one organ is often attacked by the disease, but the lungs are primarily involved for they offer ready access to inhaled bacilli. When we speak of tuberculosis, we usually mean pulmonary tuberculosis.

In the lungs of individuals with good resistance to the disease, the inhaled tubercle bacilli become surrounded by cells and are eventually walled off, neutralised rather than destroyed; clinical disease is therefore not apparent, but a very large number of bacilli or a reduction in the host's immunity or any combination of these can produce disease.

In those who are susceptible, for whatever reasons, the local reaction in the lung or other affected tissue is not contained, and the very attempts of the body to suppress the disease activity produce areas of tissues - lungs - in which the supply of blood has been cut off. Eventually this produces tissue death. Sooner or later the patient's cough - a feature of the disease - removes some of this dead lung tissue leaving holes or cavities within the lungs which is a major characteristic of pulmonary tuberculosis. In this process of cavitation, attempts at repair of the damaged tissue goes on at the same time as new lung is being invaded and destroyed. At some stage in the course of this pathological process, blood vessels in the affected lungs will be eroded leading to bleeding into the air spaces and cavities. This may be a trivial affair, with a little blood-streaking of the sputum, but there can be a major haemorrhage - termed haemoptysis. It is usually repetitive and it is easy to see why it is such a common feature of pulmonary tuberculosis. Haemoptysis may be a dramatic event, and is the one which often brings the patient to a doctor.

There is something very strange about immunity to tuberculosis. For the individual not only the obvious features relating to nutritional state and the possibility of close contact with other infected people are involved, there is community or herd immunity or even family immunity. It seems that the experience of tuberculosis of a community or race can be reflected in the types of disease manifestations which are commonly encountered at a particular time. Thus in England at the beginning of the 19th century not only was tuberculosis an extremely common illness but it produced a form of florid disease spreading rapidly and widely in the lungs, so that without specific treatment, death was almost inevitable. Tuberculosis accounted for a fair proportion of the high infant mortality, for when a young child acquired the infection there was often generalised spread to involve many sites, and death from tuberculous meningitis was common. Those who survived into adult life became susceptible in their late teens and early adult life to the classical wasting form of the disease or phthisis. This picture of the 'consumptive' is well recognised in literature. The question is raised, is there such a thing as a consumptive type? Lord Brock in his Sydenham lecture on Keats's last illness, debates this point and tends to come down against the proposition that there is a consumptive type. It is impossible to be dogmatic where the interplay of so many variables is at work - general state of the subject, number of organisms involved, the virulence of these organisms, previous experience of the organism and opportunity for repeated exposure, particularly in crowded close living conditions.

An idea of the prevalence and severity of tuberculosis in Keats's time can be obtained when we realise that in London 1801 one third of all deaths were ascribed to tuberculosis. Today the picture has changed dramatically. Recognition of the aetiological agent - 'Koch's bacillus' - in 1882 followed in 1895 by Röntgen's discovery of X-Rays, led to the two major diagnostic techniques which when fully employed allowed whole populations to be surveyed; sputum examination and radiology remain very much part of the modern means of control of tuberculosis. The development of skin tests (Mantoux test) to assess the patient's possible previous experience of tubercle bacilli and the production of a vaccine (B.C.G.) which when given to subjects provides a measure of immunity, without causing disease, were two other major developments in diagnosing and preventing the illness. Treatment of the individual patient however, even after the infectious nature of the condition was recognised, was unsatisfactory. He was isolated to keep him from infecting others and little more than rest and good diet, which were considered in some general way to be helpful, were the major features of what might be called the sanatorium way of life. In the lungs, attempts were made to rest the diseased part and to close cavities in order to shorten the process of healing. To accomplish this, a variety of forms of 'collapse' therapy were introduced, the best known of which is probably the injection of air into the pleural space, that is, artificially inducing a pneumothorax. This air had to be replaced at regular intervals.

Later, with improvements in anaesthetic and surgical techniques, a variety of operations were devised, often of a mutilating nature, in which diseased lungs or parts of lungs were renovated or removed. These surgical measures merely indicated the way in which medical treatment had failed to arrest or cure the disease, and this unsatisfactory situation obtained until the whole picture was dramatically altered by the introduction of effective antituberculous chemotherapy. To say that these drugs have revolutionised the outlook of this disease, responsible for death, misery and so much suffering, is not to overstate the case. The first antibiotic - penicillin - introduced in the 1940's, did not have activity against the tubercle bacillus, but in 1949 streptomycin, discovered by Waxman, came into use and was found to have antituberculous activity. Used on its own it sometimes cured patients but many bacilli became resistant to its action and it was not until other effective agents - PAS and isoniazid - were used in conjunction with streptomycin, that a really effective curative drug regime was worked out. Many other compounds have been isolated, and happily, today we have a dozen or so powerful weapons at our disposal. Treatment has become shorter, simpler, less tedious but above all curative.

In England today the incidence of tuberculosis is very low and the general population is scarcely aware that it still exists and can cause disease in some vulnerable members of the population; there is a much higher incidence in Asian and African immigrants. If one looks at the graph of the incidence of this disease, one is of course impressed by the changes in the past twenty years or so, but extraordinarily the slope of the graph has been downward for at least one hundred years, indicating that social and possibly nutritional factors have been a major influence on the incidence of tuberculosis. Today we are reaping the combined benefits of social improvements, medical understanding and the chemotherapeutic revolution. To some extent these generally satisfactory trends, have been halted, or even reversed by the evolution of antibiotic - resistant bacilli particularly in communities with a high incidence of AIDS.

Returning now to Keats, consider for a moment those in his immediate environment, particularly his family who were afflicted with tuberculosis. His uncle Midgley John Jennings commissioned as second lieutenant in the navy in 1796 became ill in 1807. Soon he was spitting blood and died the following year. At the time of his death Keats was about 12. Two years later his mother died. It is always assumed that she died from tuberculosis, the cause of her death being described as a 'decline', which term was often used euphemistically for tuberculosis.

Keats was very close to his brothers, especially Tom, of whom we have few details except in regard to his illness and ultimate death from tuberculosis. To celebrate Tom's 17th birthday - November 18th, 1816, John wrote a sonnet, touching and tragic when one knows the fate of both brothers:

> This is your birth-day Tom and I rejoice
> That thus it passes smoothly, quietly.
> Many such eves of gently whisp'ring noise
> May we together pass, and calmly try
> What are this world's true joys, - ere the great voice
> From its fair face, shall bid our spirits fly.

Tom may have spent some time in France but by early 1817 he was in Hampstead with his brothers, and it is thought his illness dates from about that period. In December George took Tom to Teignmouth in Devon for a change of air and in March of the following year John joined

Tom at the harbour resort. He found Tom improved in health and much taken by his medical attendant, Dr William Turton, who had made a special study of his disease. But by March 13th we find Keats right at the end of his letter to Bailey saying:-

> My brother Tom desires to be remember'd to you - he has just this moment had a spitting of blood poor fellow ...

Tom's condition became worse and they cut short their stay in Devon. It was a long unpleasant journey back to London; at Bridport Tom lost a quantity of blood.

Tom and John returned to Hampstead in early May. Later in the month George married Georgiana Wylie and the young couple made plans to emigrate to America. Thus John had the illness of one brother and the imminent departure of the other on his mind. He was at this time also much taken up with the preparations for the walking tour of Scotland with Brown.

John had become friendly with Charles Dilke and Charles Armitage Brown who shared a house, Wentworth Place on the edge of Hampstead Heath. Brown was to become one of Keats's greatest friends and at this time visits to Wentworth Place must have been a welcome change from the lodgings up the hill at Well Walk.

Tom's condition must have given some cause for concern but nevertheless he was left in charge of Mrs Bentley, their landlord's wife while John and Brown went to Scotland.

Eventually a party of four, Keats, Brown, George and Georgiana set out by coach on June 22nd for Liverpool. This was to be the port of embarkation for the young married couple while Keats and Brown made the journey the first leg of their trip to Scotland. We know that on returning from Scotland John took on the detailed day-to-day nursing of Tom, whose condition had further deteriorated. To Dilke, recuperating in Hampshire after an illness, he summarises the position in his letter:

> I wish I could say Tom was any better. His identity presses upon me so all day that I am obliged to go out - and although I intended to have given some time to study alone, I am obliged to write, and plunge into abstract images to ease myself of his countenance his voice and feebleness - so that I live now in a continual fever - it must be poisonous to life although I feel well.

As Tom's condition continued to deteriorate, friends offered to relieve Keats's vigil - Severn volunteered to let him have a night or two off but Keats continued by his failing brother's side. Tom died on December 1st and was buried on the 7th. On hearing the news, Brown suggested to Keats that he should have nothing more to do with his lodgings in Well Walk and that he should come to live with him at Wentworth Place. Keats replied: 'I think it would be better'.

Of George Keats we know that having emigrated to America, he returned once to England, and that in his mid-forties he too died from tuberculosis.

One other victim of tuberculosis, not a family member, with whom Keats had contact is Miss Cotterell. She was a young woman, about Keats's age, who with her friend Mrs Pidgeon, shared the voyage to Rome on the *Maria Crowther* with Keats and Severn. Miss Cotterell, a pretty young woman, seems to have been in an even more advanced stage of consumption than Keats. The descriptions of the voyage are really horrific; one is amazed that either patient survived the journey. The voyage was prolonged because of severe storms in the Channel and on arrival off Naples the authorities demanded that all ships from the Port of London should be quarantined for six weeks because of an outbreak of typhus in London; the *Maria Crowther* had to wait off shore for another ten days. During the voyage Keats preferred to keep the portholes closed; if they were open they induced coughing and inevitable haemoptysis. Miss Cotterell on the other hand, liked to keep them open and if they were closed she fainted for several hours at a time. The tensions and frustrations are not difficult to imagine. Eventually they got ashore and Severn and Keats were settled in lodgings by Miss Cotterell's brother, a banker in Naples. The weather was wet and foggy. Keats tried to write a letter to Brown but after only two sentences he gave up:

'... I must go on a little; perhaps it may relieve the load of WRETCHEDNESS which presses upon me'. The word written in capitals in Keats's own hand summarises what the voyage and his illness had done to him.

To trace the course of Keats's own tuberculosis we return to the summer of 1818 when he got back to Hampstead from the walking tour with Brown. Before going up to Well Walk he looked in at Wentworth Place to see the Dilkes. Mrs Dilke was apparently amused at his shabby torn clothing 'scarcely any shoes left' but any levity in the moment of meeting must have been quickly dispelled by the Dilkes' news of Tom's poor condition.

Brown had let his half of the house during the period of the walking tour, to a widow, Mrs Frances Brawne. On hearing the bad news about Tom, Keats seems to have left immediately for Well Walk without meeting Mrs Brawne or her daughter Fanny. The Brawnes later removed to Elm Cottage in Downshire Hill very close to Wentworth Place and here Keats did meet Fanny in October or November. Fanny was eighteen, a vivacious personality with a lovely complexion; the descriptions seem to suggest that she fell just short of being beautiful. Keats and Fanny Brawne developed an intimate friendship that in the initial stages was fraught with flirtation and teasing in much the way that an affair might spring up between any young couple, but it developed into a relationship which for Keats became a dominant feature, indeed an obsession for the remainder of his short life. The poems, letters and the life all indicate the

Fanny Brawne (1800-1865) Miniature 1833. Artist unknown.

depth of his feelings, the anxieties and frustrations which he endured. And this romance with Fanny Brawne was starting up during the last few months of Tom's life.

There is a suggestion that John had not been in full health from about the end of 1817 when he comments on 'The little Mercury I have taken' and this has lent to a great deal of speculation. In February and June 1819 he comments on his curious sore throats that have never been adequately explained. His general health seems to have declined, and in December 1819 he again mentions his throat when he is 'fearful lest the weather should affect my throat which on exertion or cold continually threatens me'. Occasionally tuberculosis can cause sore throat but this occurs most often when there is florid pulmonary disease, and at the time of his complaint of sore throat, while Keats may well have been suffering from tuberculosis, it is unlikely to have advanced sufficiently far to cause throat involvement. The 'sore throat' of tuberculosis is usually a laryngitis which causes hoarseness rather than pain, and is quite unlike the intermittent symptom of which Keats complained; if hoarseness had been his complaint we should have heard of it.[18]

After Tom's death his brother's annuity was to be divided among the three remaining children. During his return visit to England George and John had some misunderstanding in the manipulation of these financial details, but some money from Tom's estate came to John and he bought himself a new greatcoat and shoes on Dr Sawrey's[19] orders to keep out the rigors of winter and to keep his sore throats at bay.

On February 3rd 1820 during a warm spell, Keats left off his greatcoat. He travelled from Town arriving cold from being on the outside of the coach. At about 11 o'clock he got out at the stop at Pond Street and stumbled into Wentworth Place. Brown saw that he was ill and advised him to go to bed immediately, which he did. Brown went to his bedroom bringing him a glass of spirits just as Keats was getting between the sheets. As he did so, Keats coughed slightly and Brown heard him say "That is blood from my mouth" as he examined a single drop on the sheet.

"Bring me the candle, Brown, and let me see this blood" and then looking up at Brown he said "I know the colour of that blood; it is arterial

---

[18] Brock has been able to trace only one reference to hoarseness namely, after the first night on board the *Maria Crowther*. See Brock's Sydenham Lecture 1973 p.8.
[19] Tom's regular physician, subsequently John's. (See Appendix I).

blood. I cannot be deceived in that colour. That drop of blood is my death warrant. I must die."

However dramatic this account is, it is also diagnostic and prognostic; and the diagnostician in this case is Keats himself. Later that night he suffered a severe haemorrhage, described in his letter to Fanny Brawne:

> On the night I was taken ill when so violent a rush of blood came to my lungs that I felt nearly suffocated - I assure you I felt it possible I might not survive and at that moment thought of nothing but you ...

Just over one year later Keats died in Rome. This year is a chronicle of the course of progressive phthisis with periods of rest induced by fever and malaise; of haemoptysis and treatments with bleeding which invariably made the situation worse; of periods of apparent improvement or even optimism - perhaps a manifestation of the euphoria that has been called the 'spes phthicia', but always with an inevitable downhill course. The description of the later phase of Keats's tuberculosis is given in the final chapter so that the biographic trend continues uninterruptedly.

In the series of letters to Fanny Brawne following his first haemorrhage, we get a good impression of how tormented Keats was by the anxieties of his illness and the emotional stress of his love for Fanny.

For Keats, now entering the last year of his life, the twin spectres that were to hound him to the end were now fully developed - his disease and his love for Fanny Brawne. The extraordinary thing is that for Keats as the end approached they become one and the same.

Probably the 4th February, that is the day after his haemorrhage, he writes:

> Dearest Fanny, I shall send this the moment you return. They say I must remain confined to this room for some time. The consciousness that you love me will make a pleasant prison of the house next to yours. You must come and see me frequently: this evening, without fail ...

On February 10th:

> My Dearest Girl -
> If illness makes such an agreeable variety in the manner of your

eyes I should wish you sometimes to be ill. I wish I had read your note before you went last night that I might have assured you how far I was from suspecting any coldness: You had a just right to be a little silent to one who speaks so plainly to you.

And later, still in February -

My sweet love, I shall wait patiently till tomorrow before I see you, and in the mean time, if there is any need of such a thing, assure you by your Beauty, that whenever I have at any time written on a certain unpleasant subject, it has been with your welfare impress'd upon my mind. How hurt I should have been had you ever acceded to what is, notwithstanding, very reasonable! How much the more do I love you from the general result! In my present state of Health I feel too much separated from you ...

And later:

My Dearest Girl,
According to all appearances I am to be separated from you as much as possible. How I shall be able to bear it, or whether it will not be worse than your presence now and then, I cannot tell ... You know our situation what hope is there if I should be recovered ever so soon - my very health with [for will] not suffer me to make any great exertion. I am reccommended not even to read poetry much less write it. I wish I had even a little hope ...

And again:

My dearest Girl, how could it ever have been my wish to forget you? how could I have said such a thing? The utmost stretch my mind has been capable of was to endeavour to forget you for your own sake seeing what a change [for chance] there was of my remaining in a precarious state of health. I would have borne it as I would bear death if fate was in that humour: but I should as soon think of choosing to die as to part from you ...

February 24th:

> My dearest Girl,
> Indeed I will not deceive you with respect to my Health. This is the fact as far as I know. I have been confined three weeks and am not yet well - this proves that there is something wrong about me which my constitution will either conquer or give way to - Let us hope for the best ...

And again in March:

> My dearest Fanny, I slept well last night and am no worse this morning for it. Day by day if I am not deceived I get a more unrestrain'd use of my Chest. The nearer a racer gets to the Goal the more his anxiety becomes so I lingering upon the borders of health feel my impatience increase. Perhaps on your account I have imagined my illness more serious than it is: how horrid was the chance of slipping into the ground instead of into your arms - the difference is amazing Love - Death must come at last; Man - must die, as Shallow says; but before that is my fate I feign would try what more pleasures than you have given so sweet a creature as you can give. Let me have another oportunity of years before me and I will not die without being remember'd. Take care of yourself dear that we may both be well in the Summer. I do not at all fatigue myself with writing, having merely to put a line or two here and there, a Task which would worry a stout state of body and mind, but which just suits me as I can do no more.
>   Your affectionate
>   J.K.

CHAPTER VI

Keats and Sexuality

From his life and his writing we know a great deal about John Keats; we marvel at the magic of his poetry and acclaim the insights and frank disclosures in his letters. We are constantly aware, amazed even, at his emotion, passion and intellect whether he is dealing with ideas, situations or people. It is therefore appropriate to examine briefly the way in which Keats came to terms with his own passionate nature, what was his attitude to women and experience of them, what was the reason for his taking 'a little mercury' - did he really have an opportunity of acquiring venereal disease? Briefly, what of Keats and sexuality?

To some of these questions there cannot be precise answers, and that may be no bad thing, but we can observe some trends or patterns which do, on the whole, make a fairly consistent picture - his attitude to women for instance.

Towards his mother Keats displayed an intense love as shown by the story of her early illness when he stood guard over her door, and later, when she was seriously ill, John appointed himself her guardian, brought her medicines and read to her for long hours. But he never refers to her in his letters; was there some traumatic experience to explain this absence? For his sister Fanny he always had a warm brotherly affection when Abbey wasn't frustrating his intentions. He certainly enjoyed the company of Georgiana Wylie who subsequently married George Keats. He respected her judgement and her detachment, but this close companionship was broken when the young couple emigrated to America, though Keats continued to write to them both in the most detailed and affectionate terms. His comments to Benjamin Bailey about Georgiana are quite revealing -

> I had known my sister in Law some time before she was my Sister and was very fond of her. I like her better and better - she is the most

> disinterested woman I ever knew - that is to say she goes beyond degree in it - To see an entirely disinterested Girl quite happy is the most pleasant and extraordinary thing in the world ...

Mary Frogley, reputed to have been 'an old flame' of Keats was a pretty girl who took an interest in his work and some of the early verses were addressed to her.

One of Keats's early friends, John Hamilton Reynolds, who had something of a literary reputation, was only a year older than Keats. He had three sisters and both George and John had easy and pleasant relations with the two elder sisters. It was through his friendship with the Reynolds family that he met their cousin, Jane Cox, whose flirtations seem to have upset the Reynolds girls. Jane was a remarkable beauty with a relaxed assurance in her attitude towards the opposite sex, precisely the sort of confidence which Keats lacked. He had written to Reynolds, now engaged -

> I have spoken to you against Marriage, but it was general, the Prospect in these matters has been to me so black that I have not been unwilling to die ...

This seems rather an excessive, perhaps histrionic expression of despair, but several months later after meeting Jane Cox, again to Reynolds he writes

> I was never in love - yet the voice and the shape of a Woman has haunted me these two days - at such a time when the relief, the feverous relief of Poetry seems a much less crime -.

Clearly Keats is taken with this attractive woman. He explains his feelings in more detail to the George Keatses -

> ... and from what I hear she is not without faults - of a real kind; but she has others which are more apt to make women of inferior charms hate her. She is not a Cleopatra, but she is at least a Charmian. She has a rich eastern look; she has fine eyes and fine manners. When she comes into a room she makes an impression the same as the Beauty of a Leopardess. She is too fine and too conscious of herself to repulse any man who may address her - from habit she thinks that nothing particular. I always find myself

more at ease with such a woman; the picture before me always gives me a life and animation which I cannot possibly feel with any thing inferior - I am at such times too much occupied in admiring to be awkward or on a tremble. I forget myself entirely because I live in her. You will by this time think I am in love with her; so before I go any further I will tell you I am not - she kept me awake one Night as a tune of Mozart's might do - I speak of the thing as a passtime and an amuzement than which I can feel none deeper than a conversation with an imperial woman the very 'yes' and 'no' of whose Lips is to me a Banquet. I dont cry to take the moon home with me in my Pocket not [for/nor] do I fret to leave her behind me. I like her and her like because one has no *sensations* - what we both are is taken for granted - You will suppose I have by this had much talk with her - no such thing - there are the Miss Reynoldses on the look out - They call her a flirt to me - What a want of knowledge? she walks across a room in such a manner that a Man is drawn towards her with a magnetic Power. This they call flirting! they do not know things. They do not know what a Woman is.

If we did not have Keats's own word for it one might have concluded that he was bowled over by Jane Cox. A better description of sexual attraction it would be hard to find.

Quite clearly the conventionality of the Reynolds sisters irritated him while Jane's sexuality excited him yet this could be taken as merely an expression of Keats's dual standard for judging women. This duality is nicely shown in his summing up to Georgiana -

> As a man in the world I love the rich talk of a Charmian; as an eternal Being I love the thought of you. I should like her to ruin me, and I should like you to save me.

In a phase of depression Keats was going through Burton's *The Anatomy of Melancholy* underlining various passages. Against the phrase 'Love universally taken, is defined to be *desire*' Keats pencilled the following annotation -

> Here is the old plague spot: the pestilence, the raw scrofula. I mean that there is nothing disgraces me in my own eyes so much as being one of a race of eyes, nose and mouth beings in a planet called the

earth who all from Plato to Wesley have always mingled goatish, winnyish, lustful love with the abstract adoration of the deity.

He gives some account of his difficulties in his relation to women to Bailey -

> I am certain I have not a right feeling towards Women - at this moment I am striving to be just to them but I cannot - Is it because they fall so far beneath my Boyish imagination? When I was a Schoolboy I thought a fair Woman a pure Goddess, my mind was a soft nest in which some of them slept though she knew it not - I have no right to expect more than their reality. I thought them etherial above Men - I find then [for them] perhaps equal - great by comparison is very small - Insult may be inflicted in more ways than by Word or action - one who is tender of being insulted does not like to think an insult against another - I do not like to think insults in a Lady's Company - I commit a Crime with her which absence would have not known - Is it not extraordinary? When among Men I have no evil thoughts, no malice, no spleen - I can listen and from every one I can learn - my hands are in my pockets I am free from all suspicion and comfortable. When I am among Women I have evil thoughts, malice spleen - I cannot speak or be silent - I am full of Suspicions and therefore listen to no thing - I am in a hurry to be gone - You must be charitable and put all this perversity to my being disappointed since Boyhood - Yet with such feelings I am happier alone - among Crowds of men, by myself or with a friend or two - With all this trust me Bailey I have not the least idea that Men of different feelings and inclinations are more short sighted than myself - I never rejoiced more than at my Brothers Marriage and shall do so at any of my friends -. I must absolutely get over this - but how?

Indeed Keats's attitude to women had matured in that he was now able to put his feelings down and examine them. Gittings comments on the contrast between the 'coy naughtiness' of his letter to one of the Jeffery girls in June 1818, with another one about a year later in which he was able to discuss with her his position as an English poet.

From his account of his 'affair' with Mrs Isabella Jones, there is no doubt that Keats could enjoy a sexual adventure. Keats first met Mrs Jones at Hastings during a brief seaside holiday. She was attractive and vivacious, well read and talented, and Keats considered her about his own age. Soon he 'had warmed with her ... and kissed her'. The precise meaning of this is, of course, conjectural. However, he met the lady on another occasion, walking near Lamb's Conduit Street. He accompanied her on her walk to visit a friend in Islington. Afterwards they returned to her lodgings at 34 Gloucester Street, Queen Square. Her sitting room he found -

> a very tasty sort of place with Books, Pictures a bronze statue of Bonaparte. Music, aeolian Harp; a Parrot, a Linnet, a Case of choice Liqueurs & c. ... As I had warmed with her before and kissed her - I thought it would be living backwards not to do so again - she had a better taste: she perceived how much a thing of course it was and shrunk from it - not in a prudish way but in as I say a good taste. She contrived to disappoint me in a way which made me feel more pleasure than a simple Kiss could do - She said I should please her much more if I would only press her hand and go away ... I expect to pass some pleasant hours with her now and then ... I have no libidinous thought about her -

In his tragic romance with Fanny Brawne can be seen the epitome of his attitude to women and indeed to life. The first encounters were mere flirtations, 'emotional sparring', testing the ground in the early stages of the encounter, followed by development of emotion transformed into passion, frustrated by his illness and lack of money. There follows jealousy, periods of imagined coldness on her behalf all occurring at a time when the major constitutional effects of his advancing tuberculosis were beginning to make themselves felt. The culmination of these twin onslaughts is his decision to leave Fanny and go to Rome, which resulted inevitably in the terrible despair, frustration and anguish of the final phase of his life.

The resolution for Keats of his dilemma in which earthly sexual love could be fused with spiritual love embodied in his search for Beauty, is depicted in his poem *Endymion*. Written over a long period, the poem marks the transition from youthful enthusiasm to a mature, thoughtful state - in his own phrase leaving the 'Chamber of Maiden Thought'. *Endymion* is a poetic romance in which shadowy figures emerge, often in not very clear focus, against a sylvan background. The 'hero' Endymion (who is Keats) in his wanderings is given brief glimpses of Cynthia - his goddess of ethereal love:-

> O Cynthia, ten times bright and fair!
> From thy blue throne, now filling all the air,
> Glance but one little beam of temper'd light
> Into my bosom, that the dreadful might
> And Tyranny of love be somewhat scar'd!

but then there are the temptations of The Indian Maid representing sexual attraction:-

> My Indian bliss!
> My river-lilly bud! one human kiss!
> One sign of real breath - one gentle squeeze,
> Warm as a dove's nest among summer trees,

At one stage in the poem Endymion loses both Cynthia and the Maid and the ensuing conflict brings him to the 'Cave of Quietude' -

> For, never since the griefs and woes began
> Has thou felt so content: a grievous feud
> Hath led thee to this Cave of Quietude.

This is usually taken to mean that accepting the trials and tribulations endured by man, can produce a positive result with enhancement for the individual. Suffering and despair in other words, can be used for positive gain, and this theme became central to Keats's later psychological development.

But how does he resolve the apparent contradiction in man's need for sex as well as ethereal love, which by their very nature can produce anthisis, if in fact they are not mutually exclusive. He recognises that some form of discipline is called for -

> 'Mong men, are pleasures real as real may be:
> But there are higher ones I may not see,
> If impiously an earthly realm I take

but in the poem resolution is accomplished by a miracle in which the Indian maid is transformed into the Moon goddess.

Dorothy Hewlett, in what I consider an inspired interpretation of this passage, puts it thus, physical love between two controlled beings, masters of themselves, is fused with the spiritual love which is Beauty and a part of that love which passeth all understanding.

Keats always seems aware of what Ricks calls the 'ambivalence of sensation', pointing out that rich pleasure in the moment of its achievement can become a poisoned satiation[20], and quotes *'Ode to Melancholy'* -

> And Joy, whose hand is ever at his lips
> Bidding adieu; and aching pleasure nigh,
> Turning to poison while the bee-mouth sips.

In her book Dorothy Hewlett rejects the suggestion that Keats was oversexed. The only evidence she found to the contrary was one sentence in a letter to Tom:-

> With respect to Women I think I shall be able to conquer my passions hereafter better than I have yet done.

Two of the earlier poems are usually taken as evidence of sexual experience.

> I
> Unfelt, unheard, unseen,
> I've left my little queen,
> Her languid arms in silver slumber lying:
> Ah! though their nestling touch
> Who - who could tell how much
> There is for madness - cruel, or complying?
>
> II
> Those faery lids now sleek!
> Those lips how moist! they speak,
> In ripest quiet, shadows of sweet sounds:
> Into my fancy's ear
> Melting a burden dear,
> How "Love doth know no fullness nor no bounds".

---

[20] Christopher Ricks. *Keats and Embarrassment.* 1974 OUP p.144.

III

True! - tender monitors!
I bend unto your laws:
This sweetest day for dalliance was born!
So, without more ado,
I'll feel my heaven anew,
For all the blushing of the hasty morn.

Sharing Eve's Apple
I
O blush not so! O blush not so!
Or I shall think you knowing;
And if you smile the blushing while
Then maidenheads are going.

II
There's a blush for won't, and a blush for shan't,
And a blush for having done it:
There's a blush for thought and a blush for naught,
And a blush for just begun it,

V
There's a sigh for yes, and a sigh for no
And a sigh for I can't bear it!
O what can be done, shall we stay or run?
O cut the sweet apple and share it!

We have therefore some evidence that Keats had some sexual experience, that is sexual intercourse. Details of sexual matters at the best of times are notoriously unreliable and interpretations of events, poems, letters vary enormously. Despite a vast amount of interest and even with the benefit of hindsight, this unreliability is nowhere more clearly demonstrated than in the instance of Keats and venereal disease.

The modern biographer whose subjects may include well-known and often well-loved figures, may find that he has an enormous volume of material to assess; he can therefore in many cases produce detailed histories, often with documentary support, in a way that has not been attempted by, or indeed been possible, for biographers of earlier generations. One effect of reproducing such biographical minutiae is that the image of a personality which has been established by previous writers, may be altered in a way which some may not find acceptable. Something of the sort may have occurred in the case of Richard Holmes' superb chronicle of Shelley's life; the poet was shown to be quite human as well as romantic. Indeed Holmes put on display not only the finer strengths of Shelley's character but also his weakness and his more distasteful attributes.

For Keats there has been no recent relevant material to clarify any of the more controversial aspects of his life. This is most clearly demonstrated by the debate on Keats and venereal disease. The controversy has been succinctly summarised by Gittings.[21]

The problem seems to date from 1817 in Keats's much quoted letter to Bailey of October 8th, having spent some time with his friend in Oxford, Keats writes

> The little Mercury I have taken has corrected the Poison and improved my health - though I feel from my employment that I shall never again be secure in Robustness - would that you were as well as
>
> your sincere friend and brother
> John Keats.

This tantalising tit-bit has been seized upon, interpreted and re-interpreted; although the debate continues and even though it cannot now be resolved, it has a certain interest. The account which follows is based on Gittings' appendix on the subject.

In 1900 in his article in the *Asclepiad* on Keats's life based on Buxton Forman's biography and his conversations with Keats's friend Henry Stephens, Richardson states:

> In the autumn of the same year, 1817, he visits a friend, Bailey by name at Oxford, and in that visit runs loose, and pays a forfeit for his indiscretion, which ever afterwards physically and morally embarasses him.

Here is implied a sexual indiscretion, though no disease is named. Gittings points out that Richardson in this context was interpreting Keats's own words and was not quoting Stephens' account. We are

---

[21] R. Gittings: *J.K.* Heinemann. 1968. Appendix 3. p.446.

therefore dealing with Gittings' reading of Richardsons's account of Forman's interpretation of what Keats might have said.

Two other biographers are now involved in accounts based on this letter to Bailey. W.M. Rossetti (1887) repeated Keats's statement commenting that it 'speaks for itself'; in 1925 Lowell also quoted the letter and misquoted Rossetti by suggesting that Keats had acquired syphilis at Oxford. This is the first mention of syphilis. It appears to be a statement by Lowell, attributing to Rossetti a conclusion he did not express based on Richardson's interpretation of Forman's biography of Keats. Two later biographers, Hewlett and Bate, refuted the 'syphilis' theory, but a third - Ward - accepted Lowell's syphilis invention and argued that it was true. Gittings puts the whole situation in a nutshell when he says 'It would therefore seem that the hotly debated point whether Keats had or did not have syphilis is a pure invention of his biographers'.

Why then, one asks, was Keats taking mercury - a little mercury? Mercury has been used in medicine for 2,000 years or more; it is mentioned about 315 B.C. in Greek writing by Theophrastus and may well have been used by the Chinese at an even earlier date. C.T. Andrews (1969) in his paper on *Keats and Mercury* points out that the Guy's Hospital pharmacopoeia of 1818 lists 30 different mercurial preparations; it was used in the treatment of conditions as diverse as hydrocephalus, hemiplegia, chronic hepatitis and tabes mesenterica. There is no doubt that in Keats's time mercury was the treatment for syphilis, whatever else it may have been used for.

Gittings argues that an important distinction is to be made between 'mercury' and a 'little mercury' based on the view held by many at the time, that gonorrhoea or clap was an early stage of syphilis. The idea is invoked that a small amount, that is a little mercury, would be appropriate in the treatment of what was considered the early stages of syphilis, but what we now know to be an entirely different infection - namely gonorrhoea.[22] The dangers of using large doses of mercury were fairly well known and some doctors at this time might very well have used small doses even for syphilis, as recommended by no less an authority than Astley Cooper.

---

[22] Gonorrhoea (G) and Syphilis (S) are both acquired almost exclusively by sexual contact. G is common, easily treated and today not often followed by permanent sequelae. S, even today, although treatable and curable, is a serious infection which may have manifestations in many body systems, and can result in permanent disability.

Gittings cites Keats's doctor, S. Sawrey, who had produced a treatise on *An Inquiry into the Effects of the Venereal Poison* in which Sawrey indicates that the use of mercury should be confined to treating syphilis and that small doses should be used in the early stages (i.e. gonorrhoea) and large doses for the later stages of syphilis.

Gittings' conclusion, which in my view cannot be gainsaid on present evidence, is that Sawrey was treating Keats at this time for gonorrhoea, with a little mercury. He also supports his conclusion by reference to Keats's comment about a year later that while under 'Sawrey's Mandate' he was taking mercury in sufficiently large doses to cause nervousness. This is interpreted as confirmation that Sawrey believed the earlier treatment was for gonorrhoea while the later malady - possibly the sore throat on his return from the Scottish walking tour - might have been a manifestation of syphilis.

Nothing more conclusive on the subject can be said at this stage of our knowledge.

Keats House (present day).

CHAPTER VII

Finale

At the time of his first haemorrhage Keats was sharing one half of Wentworth Place with Brown. The other half had been vacated by Dilke when he moved into central London to be near his son who was attending Westminster School. Dilke's half of the house was rented to Mrs Brawne and her daughter Fanny. The house, now called Keats House, at that time had, with the exception of two half-built houses, a clear view of open heath, so that Keats was able to see and to describe the comings and goings on the heath. This he did in a charming letter to Fanny Keats. Today the house is still a beautiful, quiet place to visit where a special library devoted to Keats is housed and many other memorabilia may be seen. The picture shows Keats House in Summer 1982.

The maid, Ann, who had looked after Keats and Brown had been replaced by an Irish girl called Abigail O'Donaghue. Soon Brown was sleeping with her and Abigail became pregnant. Brown was a very cautious man with money; he always shared his house and eked out his slender means by letting his house when he went away for any length of time. When he and Keats were housekeeping together, Keats paid Brown five pounds a month. These domestic arrangements worked well enough as long as Keats was able to pay his share of the costs, but in his reduced circumstances after giving George so much of his capital, he was forced to borrow from Brown. Moreover, Brown felt that he had claims of friendship on Keats that may have been no more than 'protective', but he positively resented the intrusion of Fanny Brawne. To upset the young couple's relationship Brown at one stage flirted with Fanny, and an awkward, ill-tempered, three cornered arrangement existed for some time. Despite all this, Brown was, in the main, a devoted nurse to Keats in his illness, and allowing for a certain coarseness, Keats was lucky in having such a practical organiser in the same house.

On the night of his haemoptysis, Brown had called Dr G.R. Rodd, the surgeon of Hampstead High Street. Treatment as recommended at the time consisted of bleeding, rest and what amounted to a starvation diet. Tom, complaining about his dietary management had written to Dilke that invalids 'are supposed to have delicate stomachs; and for my part I should like a slice of underdone sirloin'.

Bleeding as a form of treatment deserves some consideration, especially as we view it with such scepticism in contemporary medicine, although it may be said to have one or two legitimate indications. Why one asks, was it regarded as such a panacea for all ills? - the modern sceptic replies - 'because there was nothing better to offer'. But the position is not quite so simple.

The origins of the usefulness of bleeding or venesection are lost in antiquity.[23] The idea that bleeding could improve bodily ills may have been chanced upon by early man in observing bleeding after injury. There may also have been a link with the idea of cleansing the body of noxious substances as with the regular bleeding of menstruation. The early Egyptians only permitted two surgical procedures - circumcision and venesection. The Babylonians tried to make special inferences from the appearance of the blood drawn at venesection. There are no references to bloodletting in the Bible but at the time of the 2nd century AD during the preparation of the Hebrew Law book - the *Talmud* - we learn that bleeding was well known.

The Hindus, perhaps as a result of Alexander's Indian expedition of 327 BC, were probably influenced by Greek practice, and the *Susruta* - the major reference work on Indian surgery, indicates familiarity with surgical technique and surgical instruments including lancets, scalpels and forceps. The Hindus taught blood letting by practising on plants and cadavers before approaching patients. This is very similar to modern views on learning in invasive medical techniques. Hippocrates is worth quoting in his teaching on bleeding.[24]

> Bleed in the acute affections, if the disease appears strong, ...

> Peripneumonia and pleuritic affections are thus to be observed: If the fever be acute with pains on either side or both, if expiration be painful, if cough be present and the sputa yellow or livid in colour

---

[23] See: Garrison, F.H. *The History of Bloodletting* 1913. New York Medical Journal, Vol. 97. pp.432-7; 498-501.
[24] See: *Hippocrates: Genuine Works* translated by Francis Adams. New York 1886.

or otherwise thin, frothy and florid, let the physician proceed thus: If the pain pass upward to the clavicle, the breast or the arm, the inner vein in the arm should be opened on the affected side, the blood abstracted according to the habit, age and complexion of the patient and the season of the year, and that largely and boldly, if pain be acute, so as to bring on fainting, after which a clyster[25] is to be given.

Who could argue with venesection as a treatment to be recommended in acute chest illness after such an instruction from the founder of European medicine.

Celsus, born towards the end of the reign of Augustus and still living in the time of Caligula, begins his chapter on blood letting:[26]

> It is not a new practice to let blood by the incision of a vein but it is new to embrace this remedy in almost every disease.

Subsequently great controversy ensued on the relative merits of bleeding on the affected side or the opposite side as favoured by Arabic practitioners; the frequency of venesection and the quantity of blood to be removed was fertile ground for argument.

Galen advised that the usual quantity to be removed was 7oz. to $1\frac{1}{2}$ lbs. Sydenham, a pioneer English clinician, venesected for most conditions but removed very little blood.

Harvey's work on the circulation had no appreciable effect on blood letting and it was left to Magendie to point out that the effects of venesection were the same at whatever point the blood was removed.

Medieval medicine under the Christian Church had its origins in the School of Salernum which produced the *Regimen Sanitatis*, a 12th century Code of Health in the form of a poem composed for King Robert of Normandy who was cured of a wound in Salerno in 1101. A single couplet gives the flavour:

> Bleeding soothes rage, brings joy unto the sad
> And saves all lovesick swains from going mad.

Clearly venesection had now become prophylactic as well as therapeutic.

---

[25] Clyster: an enema.
[26] *Celsus, On Medicine*. Trans. A.Lee. London 1981. pp. 99-106.

Blood letting became extraordinarily popular in Europe in the 15th and 16th centuries. It was often carried out in the public baths where the bath keeper was a barber-surgeon. Blood letting calendars were printed in Mainz in 1462.

In the first half of the 19th century venesection was carried on extensively and intensively. When in 1844 Flaubert had his first fit, his brother - a doctor - bled him. An English Quaker practitioner, John Coakley Lettson, had an epigram made about him:

> When patients sick to me apply,
> I purges, bleeds and sweats 'em:
> If after that they choose to die,
> What's that to me? I Lettsom.

The bleeding and dietary restriction imposed on Keats, orthodox enough at the time, could only have made his general condition worse. His physical illness - that is his tuberculosis and its treatment - was compounded by frustration in his love for Fanny Brawne, anxiety over Fanny's relations with Brown, and possibly resentment at Brown's sexual freedom with Abigail - a freedom which convention denied to himself and Fanny. Add to all this the problems relating to his work in preparing another volume of poems for publication as well as his straightened pecuniary circumstances, and we have what even today would be a formidable problem in medical management.

On March 6th - just over a month after his initial haemoptysis - Keats was afflicted by severe palpitations. In despair he took to his bed for two days; Brown wrote to his publisher Taylor, saying that the revision of the poems would have to be put off indefinitely. Dr Rodd was now his regular physician and it was probably he who arranged for Keats to be seen by a specialist. Dr Robert Bree was a distinguished chest physician with a special interest in asthma, on which subject he had produced one of the standard works. He had suffered from asthma himself and counted among his patients the Duke of Sussex, son of George III. Now aged about 60 and at the height of his career, he examined Keats, almost certainly without the aid of a stethoscope, for it was only in the previous year that Laennec had introduced it in Paris.

In 1816 René Laennec working at the Necker Hospital in Paris, became familiar with immediate auscultation (i.e. direct application of the ear to the chest) as a method of clinical examination. The circumstances that led to *mediate* auscultation, that is the discovery of the stethoscope, can be told in Laennec's own words.

> In 1816 I was consulted by a young woman presenting general symptoms of diseases of the heart. The patient's age and sex did not permit me to resort to the kind of examination I have just described [immediate auscultation], I recalled a well known acoustic phenomenon: namely, if you place your ear against one end of a wooden beam, the scratch of a pin at the other extremity is most distinctly audible. It occurred to me that this physical property might serve a useful purpose in the case with which I was then dealing. Taking a sheet of paper I rolled in into a very tight roll, one end of which I placed over the praecordial region, whilst I put my ear to the other. I was both surprised and gratified at being able to hear the beating of the heart with much greater clearness and distinctness than I had ever done by direct application of the ear.[27]

The stethoscope evolved from this primitive tightly rolled sheet of paper to a wooden model that survived in modified form up to the end of the 19th century. Laennec used his invention to study chest disease and to relate his clinical observations to the pathological findings at post-mortem examination. The culmination of this work was the publication in 1819 of one of the classics of medical literature 'De l'Auscultation Mediate, etc.'[28]

One of those most interested in the new invention was James Clark who had visited Laennec at the Necker and suggested to his friend John (later Sir John) Forbes that he should translate Laennec's work into English, and this in fact was accomplished, the first translation appearing in 1821.

Clark did later refer patients from Rome to Laennec and in a letter dated 1823 referring a Mr Gifford, there are two important comments by Clark.

> Though in the frequent habit of using the stethoscope, I have not as yet acquired sufficient confidence in my diagnostic faculty to satisfy me, though I hope soon to do so ... I have a stethoscope and

---

[27] P.J. Bishop. *Evolution of the Stethoscope*. J.Roy.Soc.Med. 1980. 73. p.448.
[28] See Sekula, A. *R.T.H. Laennec 1781-1826*. Thorax 1981, 36 p.81.
  also: P.J. Bishop. *Leannec: a great student of tuberculosis*. 1981, 62, P.129.

> have endeavoured to make its utility generally known in Italy as
> I was the first to do in England ...

From this we see that by 1823 Clark was in the habit of using the stethoscope though not quite confident in his ability to make the best of it.

Earlier in the same letter, in reference to Mr Gifford whom he was sending for Laennec's opinion regarding a chest complaint, Clark says

> the pain was perhaps more obstinate, after the symptoms of fever had disappeared than is common, and it did also appear to me that the deranged functions of the digestive organs had a considerable share in producing and keeping up the affection of the chest ...

The similarity between Clark's assessment of Keats's abdominal complaint in regard to the over-riding importance of the chest condition and that of Mr Gifford is obvious.

Despite the fact that stethoscopes were on sale in London in November 1819, the general public had no information about these medical advances, and this is well exemplified by a note from *The Times* of December 19th 1824, which was probably the first notice the lay public in England had about the stethoscope.

> A wonderful instrument called the Stethoscope, invented a few months ago for the purpose of ascertaining the different stages of pulmonary affections, is now in complete vogue at Paris. It is merely a hollow wooden tube, about a foot in length (a common flute, with the holes stopped and the top open would do, perhaps, just as well). One end is applied to the breast of the patient, the other to the ear of the physician, and according to the different sounds, harsh, hollow, soft, loud etc., he judges of the state of the disease. It is quite a fashion if a person complains of a cough, to have recourse to the miraculous tube, which, however, cannot effect a cure; but should you unfortunately perceive in the countenance of the Doctor, that he fancies certain symptoms exist, it is very likely that a nervous person might become seriously indisposed and convert the supposition into reality.

The stethoscope was a major influence in medicine in that it led to an appraisal of methods available for clinical examination, so that the earlier *technique* and little known method of percussion introduced in 1761 by Auenbrugger in combination with the new *instrument* produced by Laennec, evolved to the methods which are standard in clinical medicine today.

Bree was impressed by Keats's mental affliction and considered his illness, particularly the palpitations, a psychosomatic manifestation, a reaction to his earlier blood spitting which had induced asthma. This in itself might not be an unreasonable summary of the situation, but nothing seems to have been said of his major physical disease. With Keats's family history and given that even if the diagnosis could not be proved, tuberculosis must have been suspected by Dr Bree. It may have been, but he does not seem to have said so. The difficulties of the diagnosis could not be proved, tuberculosis must have been suspected by Dr Bree. The problems of the diagnosis of early tuberculosis are well known but this was a case in which if an X-ray had been available, it must have shown a pulmonary infiltration, possibly with cavitation. A personal recollection of my own student days comes to mind. A young man was referred to the medical outpatient department because of haemoptysis. I obtained a history of the illness and examined the patient (with the aid of a stethoscope) and found no physical abnormality. On reporting this to the consultant in charge, my lack of skill was not applauded, but I felt somewhat comforted when on examination of the patient the consultant also failed to demonstrate abnormal findings in the chest. An X-ray of the chest was taken and showed an opacity containing a cavity, subsequently proved to be tuberculous, at the apex of one lung. Having seen the X-ray abnormality, I again immediately re-examined the patient's chest, using all the tricks I was aware of including pressing my stethoscope on to that part of the chest wall under which I knew the cavity lay. I detected nothing abnormal; I did not hear any of the sounds which infiltration and cavitation may produce on auscultation.

Whatever may be the truth of Bree's diagnosis, Keats's condition improved with some return of confidence; Bree allowed him a normal diet and even some wine.

As his condition improved he continued his preparation of the 1820 volume of poems. He had happier relations with Fanny and he was able to spend more time in her company when Brown was out of the way.

On March 25th, he was well enough to attend the private viewing of his friend Haydon's painting 'Christ's Entry into Jerusalem'. This huge picture in which Keats's head appeared, was exhibited in the Egyptian Hall, Piccadilly. This was a grand occasion attended by 'the ministers and their ladies, all the foreign ambassadors, all the bishops, all the beauties in high life ... all the geniuses in town, and everybody of any note'.[29] Mrs Siddons, in case there were any doubters, declared 'It is completely successful'. Keats met Hazlitt, and seems to have enjoyed himself enormously. He walked back to Wentworth Place apparently no worse for his exertion.

Brown was as usual on the look out for a little more money and was anxious to let his house earlier than usual during his planned absence in Scotland; also, he was soon to have the increased responsibility of his child by Abigail. He also tried on Keats's behalf, to get some money from George in America. Precisely what Keats was to do when the house was let for the summer does not seem to have been discussed openly. By a stroke of luck Leigh Hunt, having himself removed to Kentish Town, undertook to find Keats cheap lodgings nearby, and on May 4th Keats moved into his new abode at No. 2 Wesleyan Place just around the corner from Hunt's lodgings. But despite Hunt's understanding, Keats was profoundly unhappy in his empty lodging house. Three extracts taken from his letters at the time to Fanny, demonstrate his predicament:-

> ... I wish you to see how unhappy I am for love of you, and endeavour as much as I can to entice you to give up your whole heart to me whose whole existence hangs upon you.

and,

> I have been a walk this morning with a book in my hand, but as usual I have been occupied with nothing but you: I wish I could say in an agreeable manner. I am tormented day and night. They talk of my going to Italy. 'Tis certain I shall never recover if I am to be so long separate from you: ... Past experience connected with the fact of my long separation from you gives me agonies which are scarcely to be talked of.

and later from the same letter

> I appeal to you by the blood of that Christ you believe in: Do not write to me if you have done anything this month which it would

---

[29] Haydon Autobiography, 1927. p.241.

have pained me to have seen. You may have altered - if you have not - if you still behave in dancing rooms and other societies as I have seen you - I do not want to live - if you have done so I wish this coming night may be my last.

These letters with an hallucinatory, almost frightening quality, reflect his diseased and anguished mind.

A letter from George in America, telling Keats of his little niece's grave illness, and without any promise of money, and this, together with an urgent call from Fanny Keats in Walthamstow, possibly in revolt against Abbey's tyrannies, did not augur tranquility. Keats had another haemoptysis and others followed. He was taken in by Leigh Hunt and met there Mrs Maria Gisborne - Shelley's friend. At this stage two other doctors were involved in Keats's care - Dr William Lambe and Dr George Darling.

Dr Lambe who lived in Kentish Town, had attended Hunt and Shelley and was something of an eccentric; he was an albino and he was a strong advocate of vegetarianism. He was not a general practitioner and had written on consumption.

Dr George Darling of Russell Square, recommended by Haydon, had attended many of Keats's friends. There is not complete agreement on which doctor was consulted first, but the differing accounts[30] do agree that at this time both physicians were involved in the management of Keats's illness. There seems to have been agreement on the diagnosis, treatment (more bleedings were undertaken) and the prognosis - the only hope for the patient was to winter in Italy.

If this is correct, and there is no reason for doubt, it is important, for the diagnosis now seems at last to have been settled, and this makes Dr Clarke's assessment in Rome all the more difficult to understand.

At no stage, in any of the accounts which I have consulted, have I been able to ascertain if anyone, physician or other, actually discussed Keats's illness with him in factual terms, or explained what they thought the likely outcome. The patient seems to have been left out of all discussion. The implications are clear enough; the patient is seriously ill and the doctors agree the only hope lies in moving to Italy; therefore one is expected to conclude that the consumption had reached a very advanced stage. But there is an indirectness of approach, despite good contemporary

---

[30] See Gittings. *J.K.* p.399.

reports including Keats's own letters, consistently present throughout the whole illness, so that it is impossible to be sure if this imprecision results from a genuine failure of both physicians and friends to discuss the illness candidly with the patient, or whether we just do not have sufficient documentation. I suspect the former is more likely, conforming to the practice of the time. The idea of what today we would call 'patient education' was totally lacking even when the patient was himself a physician. But Keats himself must have realised what was happening to him; his own phrase epitomises the situation, 'I think there is a core of disease in me not easy to pull out'. Mrs Gisborne when she saw him on 12th July, wrote in her journal 'Keats, under sentence of death from Dr Lamb.'

At this time Keats's new volume of poetry appeared. Taylor commented

> - I am sure of this that for poetic Genius there is not his equal living, and I would compare him against any one with either Milton or Shakespeare for Beauties.

Unlike his previous publications, this volume containing among other poems '*Ode to a Nightingale*, *To Autumn*, *Isabella*, *Hyperion*, *Ode on a Grecian Urn*, was received with acclaim by the reviewers.

Still quite ill and against Hunt's pleading, he made his way back to Hampstead; in Well Walk he could not bring himself to visit his old lodgings where he had nursed Tom. He appeared at Wentworth Place distraught, exhausted, and was taken in by Mrs Brawne. He remained there for the next month, lovingly tended by Fanny and her mother.

Keats and Fanny had an arrangement, possibly a secret engagement, and several times during the early acute phase of his illness he offered to release her, but she had always refused. Now there was talk of marriage and that mother and daughter should accompany him to Italy, but nothing came or could come of this. Friends called to see him and were appalled by his appearance. He applied to Abbey for a loan to fund his projected journey but was refused. The financial situation was eased by Taylor who bought the copyright of *Lamia* for £100 which left Keats with £30 when arrears had been paid. He also arranged for a credit in Italy of one hundred and fifty pounds. Taylor was apparently prepared to take the gamble that he might eventually have some of his outlay refunded by George.

Keats's friends were keen that he should be accompanied on his journey to Italy and prompted by Haslam, this task was undertaken by the young painter Joseph Severn. Severn was the winner of the Royal

Joseph Severn (1793-1878). Self portrait aged 29.

Academy Gold Medal, had the opportunity of applying for a travelling fellowship and thus the winter in Rome might be a benefit to his painting as well as to Keats's health.

Fanny's attitude to Keats had matured during the last month at Wentworth Place. The period of nursing care produced a much more tender love than she had exhibited previously. We do not know the details of the young lovers' parting; they exchanged locks of hair and wore each other's ring. It was agreed that if Keats returned Fanny and he should be married and live with Mrs Brawne.

Keats went to Taylor at Fleet Street to make final arrangements for the publication of his poetry and also to be ready to take advantage of any change in wind or tide that might allow a change of sailing for the *Maria Crowther*.

The *Maria Crowther* set out from London Docks at 7.00 p.m. on Sunday, 17th September. Severn had come aboard but he had not yet obtained his passport; his brother Tom Severn, as well as Keats's friends Taylor, Woodhouse and Haslam were present. The whole group dined with the captain. At Gravesend Keats's friends left the boat; Severn's passport finally arrived and Miss Cotterell arrived, coming on board in time for the *Maria Crowther* to catch the evening tide. By a strange coincidence Brown returning from his Scottish holiday by a small coaster, was moored within hailing distance of the *Maria Crowther*, and even stranger, when as a result of adverse winds their ship put in at Portsmouth, Keats spent his last night in England at Bedhampton - at which time Brown was staying only ten miles away with Dilke.

The horrors of the journey have been touched upon earlier and need not detain us more here. At this time Keats wrote to Mrs Brawne:-

> I dare not fix my Mind on Fanny, I have not dared to think of her. The only comfort I have had that way has been in thinking for hours together of having the knife she gave me put in a silver-case - the hair in a Locket - and the Pocket-Book in a gold net - Show her this ...

He added a postscript,

> Good bye Fanny! God bless you.

He never wrote to Fanny again.

Eventually arriving in Rome on November 15th by way of Naples, Severn and Keats settled in lodgings in the house at the edge of the Spanish Steps which had been obtained for them in advance by Dr James Clark. Here, 26 Piazza di Spagna for just over three months was Keats's last home. It was a suitable, interesting and even pleasant place. From his small rectangular room Keats could hear Bernini's fountain in the Piazza, there was a constant buzz of noise from the markets around the square, and the steps leading up to the Church of Trinita dei Monti were brightened by flowers and lively with people. Dr James Clark was a well trained physician from Edinburgh who had settled in Rome where there was a large English colony. Subsequently Clark settled in practice in London and became physician to Queen Victoria. At court one of the ladies-in-waiting - Lady Flora Hastings, was attended by Dr Clark because of an abdominal swelling. Clark may have considered that she was pregnant and the lady was dismissed from Court, subsequently to die of a malignant ovarian cyst. It is doubtful if this was a simple mis-diagnosis. (See Appendix I.) Despite this, Clark maintained his popularity with the Royal Family and although he failed to diagnose the Prince Consort's

Spanish Steps. Engraving c.1820. The house on right of steps is No. 26. Keats's and Severn's rooms were on the 2nd floor. This is now the Keats-Shelley Memorial House.

fatal illness as typhoid fever, he was made a baronet and became F.R.S. Despite these diagnostic problems which have caught the biographer's fancy, Clark was a well intentioned kind man, who kept up to date with medical advances. His initial assessment of Keats, with whom he was impressed as a personality, was that there was more likely to be disease in the stomach than in the lung. He noted Keats's anxiety which he ascribed to concern over money. His summary was:-

> The chief part of his disease so far as I can see seems to be seated in his stomach. I have some suspicion of disease of the heart and it may be of the lungs ... If I can put his mind at ease I think he'll do well.

In a patient with advanced tuberculosis who has abdominal pain and vomiting it would be a reasonable assumption that the disease had involved the intestines. This may have been what Clark meant when he said that the seat of Keats's trouble was the stomach. It should be made

Sir James Clark (1788-1870). From *Illus. London News* (16th July 1870). Engraved from a photograph by Edwards and Butt.

clear that it has not and now cannot be substantiated that Keats did in fact have abdominal tuberculosis. What is surprising is that Clark, who had a special interest in phthisis, and presumably having been informed of his new patient's family history as well as the diagnosis of the London physicians together with the express purpose of Keats's sojourn in Rome, should come to a conclusion concentrating on stomach and mind rather than the lungs as the major site of disease.

However wrong this assessment may have been it should be made clear that even if Clark had said, as with today's methods he would have been able to, 'there are multiple confluent opacities throughout both lung fields with numerous cavities especially at the apices - consistent with far advanced tuberculosis', given the treatment at the time the outcome would not have been altered one whit. As rest figured largely in the treatment of the time, it is somewhat surprising to find that Keats was allowed up, went for a few sightseeing trips and even for a ride on horseback. Keats enjoyed a little respite and his old humour began to return, and he even penned a new poem; Severn was able to turn his attention to painting and the Art world. This period lasted for about two weeks, but on December 10th he had a severe haemorrhage followed by others; Dr Clark took eight ounces of blood from his arm.

His last known letter, to Brown, is dated 30th November. It has a philosophical acceptance of the tragic realities of his whole life -

> Tis the most difficult thing in the world for me to write a letter. My stomach continues so bad that I feel it worse on opening any book ... I have an habitual feeling of my real life having past and that I am leading a posthumous existence ... Dr Clark is very attentive to me; he says there is very little the matter with my lungs, but my stomach he says, is very bad. I am well disappointed in hearing good news from George, - for it runs in my head we shall all die young ... I can scarcely bid you good bye even in a letter. I always made an awkward bow.
> God bless you!
> John Keats.

Fever returned with delirium in which Keats raged at Severn for not allowing him access to laudanum. He stumbled about his room crying 'this day shall be my last'. In nine days he had five haemorrhages. Dr Clark came four or five times a day and put Keats on a fish diet which led Keats to accuse both his friends that they were conspiring to starve him.

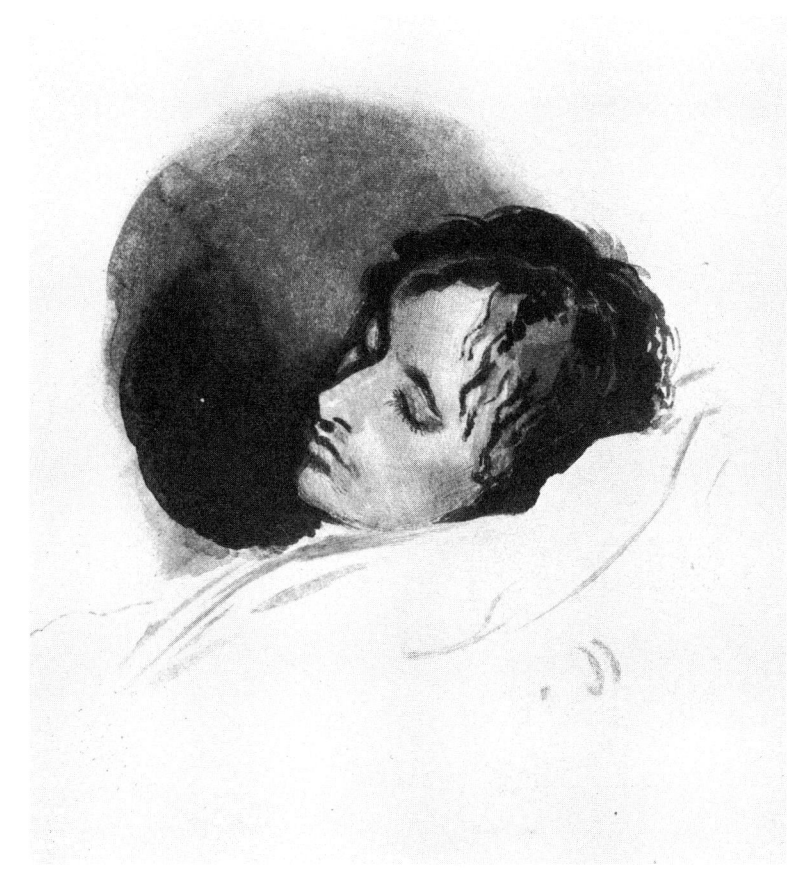

Keats on his deathbed. Joseph Severn 1821, pen and wash. Caption reads, '28 Jany, 3 o'clock mg - drawn to keep me awake - a deadly sweat was on him all this night'.

Severn was attentive and helpful but probably somewhat shocked by the vehemence of Keats's outburst in his delirious phases. On December 17th, Severn wrote -

> Not a moment I can be from him. I sit by his bed and read all day, and at night I humour him in all his wanderings. He has just fallen asleep, the first sleep for eight nights, and now from mere exhaustion.

There can be no doubt about Severn's attention, kindness and courage in looking after Keats in his last days. This is made clear in letters of the time and in the biographies - certainly so in Robert Gittings' *John Keats*, although Lord Brock in his 1971 Sydenham Lecture takes an opposite view.

Dr Clark called an Italian physician who saw Keats on Christmas Eve; neither could hold out any hope for the dying poet.

Snatches of his conversation with Severn are recorded -

> Severn, I bequeath to you all the happiness I have ever known. This is the last Christmas I shall ever see but I hope you will see many and be happy. It would be second death for me if I knew that your goodness now was your loss hereafter.

Severn, in fact, lived to be 86, became a successful painter and eventually British Consul in Rome where he died. His body was later moved to the old Protestant Cemetery where the graves of both Keats and Severn can be seen, side by side.

In the last phase of his illness there were bouts of fever, haemorrhages and occasional calm periods. Severn, hardly able to leave his dying friend's bedside, has left us a touching pen and wash sketch. Towards the very end his mind became clearer as he accepted the inevitability of death. Instead of taunting Severn about his belief in Christianity he was able to discuss his burial place, asked that Fanny Brawne's letters should be placed in his grave and that his headstone should simply bear the words 'Here lies one whose name was writ in water'.

In his last days it seemed as if Keats was having to act out a macabre version of his own belief that suffering and despair could be used to good purpose. God knows he suffered enough, but to what end? In an extraordinarily prescient comment Matthew Arnold expressed this view in a letter to Sidney Colvin, discussing the latter's first Keats biography of 1887.

'If Keats could have lived he could have done anything; *but he could not have lived*, his not living we must consider, was more than an accident.[31]'

Unlike Endymion, there was no magic solution for Keats in which two opposites could be marvellously transmogrified into something different. His condition deteriorated inexorably. He became aware of Severn's ordeal in watching him die. Just for a moment or two in the last

---

[31] *The Colvins and their Friends*. E.V. Lucas. 1928. p.194.

hours of his life his medical training asserts itself again when he looks on himself as a patient with an objective eye of a physician instructing his juniors, when he says to Severn - 'Did you ever see anyone die; well then I pity you poor Severn. Now you must be firm for it will not last long'. Later on the afternoon of February 23rd Keats called:

> Severn - Severn lift me up for I am dying - I shall die easy - don't be frightened - thank God it has come.

He died in Severn's arms a few hours later.

Two days later Dr Clark, in the presence of an Italian surgeon and a Dr Luby[32] performed a post-mortem examination. This seems to have been a limited examination probably confined to the thorax, so that we have no information on the state of the abdominal organs, the condition of the larynx or other organs that might have been affected by disease. No formal autopsy report exists as almost certainly none was made, so that our information in this respect is entirely dependent on two rather inadequate letters of Severn. Writing to John Taylor, Severn states[33]

> On Sunday the Second day Dr Clark and Dr Luby with an Italian Surgeon - opened the body - they thought it the worst possible Consumption - the lungs were virtually destroyed - the cells were quite gone - but Doctor Clark will write you on this head-

Similarly Severn writes to Brown[34]

> ... On Sunday his body was opened; the lungs were completely gone, the doctors could not conceive how he had lived in the last two months. Dr Clark will write you on this head ...

The similarity of phraseology in both letters promising Clark's future communication, suggests that there had been some discussion between Severn and Clark agreeing that the medical details should be given to Keats's friends by his physician.

---

[32] See Appendix I.
[33] *Letters of J.K.* Rollins II. p.379.
[34] *Life and Letters of Joseph Severn*. Low, Marston & Co. London 1892. p.94.

We know that Brown never received Severn's letter, for it was found, unposted, in the latter's papers; we do not know if Clark conveyed the autopsy details either to Taylor or to Brown. Many of Brown's documents were given to Monckton Milnes in order to prepare the first biography of Keats, and these papers are held at the Houghton Library in Harvard. They do not contain the letter from Clark.

If John Taylor received such a letter it is likely that he would have made some reference to it in the copious correspondence[35] he conducted with family and friends during this period. Keats's death is brought into this correspondence but nowhere is there mention of the autopsy details, and there is no letter from Clark. All of this suggests that Taylor never received Clark's letter promised by Severn even if Clark had in fact written it.

There is one other piece of evidence suggesting, but not proving, that Taylor did not receive Clark's autopsy details. Taylor it seems, on terms of some intimacy with Isabella Jones, sent her some of his letters relating to Keats's last days. In her reply, dated April 14th 1821, she goes out of her way to censure Severn for what she regarded as his egotism and selfishness, but there is no mention of any letter from Clark. Such a letter, containing the autopsy report, is unlikely to have escaped at least some mention, however unwelcome and unfortunate its medical contents.

Keats was buried on Monday 26th February; in the coffin were unopened letters of Fanny Brawne and Fanny Keats. When news of his death reached England three weeks later, Brown was astonished at the fortitude shown by Fanny, but later she wrote 'I have not got over it and never shall'. She later married Louis Lindo, twelve years younger than herself, who adopted the name Lindon; they lived mostly abroad but eventually she returned to England and was buried in Brompton Cemetery in December 1865.

My own view is that Keats's work is not as generally known or appreciated today as many believe; it is impossible to be dogmatic, and any opinion may be suspect because of its subjectivity, but if we accept Bridges' assessment that Keats is second only to Shakespeare, there seems to me an enormous gap between what many people know of Shakespeare and their knowledge of Keats. Some of his poems are well known and there will always be a few readers who will love and

---

[35] Bakewell MS. No. D504 & D1561. Held at Matlock.

understand his works, but the major study of his writing has become an academic exercise, almost an intellectual game. In Keats we are lucky to have three marvellously detailed aspects of his existence; we have his poetry, his letters and his life. I consider much of his poetry difficult but the gold is there although it may have to be sought diligently; his letters on the other hand, have an instant appeal, are a glory to read and are an astonishing statement of Keats's own philosophy, dealing not only with comments on everyday happenings but also amounting to what might be called a system of aesthetics. And of course we have numerous biographies.

When I set out to write this book I had the notion that I would find medicine had very little to do with Keats's life, especially in that he quite clearly *chose* literature, but as I progressed, my view altered and I think one can see an alteration in Keats's own attitude even in the short period of his sad life. This might be summed up by saying that we don't know why he became an apprentice, but, having reached Guy's he was interested enough to continue his medical studies, pursuing them to obtain his qualification, and that at this stage he decided firmly against surgery while leaving the door just open, or at least not locked, against medicine. Then follows his life in poetry which included some examples of medical reference and usage. Then the all-too-short life becomes a tragic case history progressing inexorably in medical content which finally excludes all other aspects of his life.

The last word must rest with Shelley. Shelley who was not particularly friendly to Keats during his life but grew to appreciate him as a poet, and produced the fine elegy - *Adonais* - after his death. We must recall that when Shelley's body was washed up on the coast after he had been drowned in the Gulf of Spezia, the pocket of his jacket was found to contain Hunt's copy of Keats's poems, folded back at *Lamia*. In *Adonais* Shelley wrote:

> Here pause: these graves are all too young as yet
> To have outgrown the sorrow which consigned
> Its charge to each; and if the seal is set,
> Here, on one fountain of a mourning mind,
> Break it not thou! too surely shalt thou find
> Thine own well full, if thou returnest home,
> Of tears and gall. From the world's bitter wind
> Seek shelter in the shadow of the tomb.
> What Adonais is, why fear we to become?

APPENDIX I

Keats's Doctors

Sawrey, Solomon (1765-1825)   27, Bedford Row. Tom's physician, also Keats's. Probably prescribed mercury for Keats (1818) in the treatment of presumed venereal disease on which subject he had produced a treatise.

Rodd, George Ramsay   Surgeon of Hampstead High Street. Called by Brown to see Keats on night of first haemoptysis (Feb. 3rd 1820). His bill for attending Keats on this and subsequent visits was £13.11s. which Charles Brown did not settle until 6th March 1821. Rodd's wife was said to be a dear friend of Fanny Brawne's.

Bree, Robert   Born in Solihull, son of medical practitioner. Educated in Coventry and matriculated at University College, Oxford 6th April 1775; M.D. July 1791. He was admitted Extra-Licentiate of Coll. of Phys. on July 31st 1781. He settled in Northampton and was appointed physician to the General Infirmary, later moving to Leicester Infirmary. Here he had a successful practice but became afflicted with asthma and because of its severity withdrew from practice in 1793. Later returned to practice in Birmingham, was appointed there to the General Hospital and published his book on asthma. He was consulted by the Duke of Sussex and on his advice removed to London where in 1806 he was admitted to Fellowship of Coll. of Phys. He

Bree, Robert - cont'd. was called to see Keats, probably by Rodd, because of Keats's palpitations. Bree died, aged 80, on 6th October 1839 at his home in Park Square, Regent's Park.

Lambe, William Born Feb. 1765 at Warwick, son of an attorney in the town. Educated at Hereford Grammar School and St. John's Coll. Camb. subsequently becoming fellow of the College. M.D. 1802. He set up in practice in Warwick and made a minute examination of the mineral water at Leamington on which he published a paper: he also published a similar study on the Thame's water. Fell. of Coll. Phys. 1804 and was Censor for 4 years, Croonian lecturer on 4 occasions, and Harveian orator in 1818. He was something of an eccentric, a confirmed vegetarian. He was an albino. He was friendly with Shelley and Hunt. Lambe saw Keats in Hunt's home in Kentish Town almost certainly in consultation with Darling (June 1820). Lambe was an accomplished, benevolent man, who never had any considerable practice of a remunerative character. He died at Dilwyn, aged 82, on 11th June 1847 and was buried in the family vault.

Darling, George Born in Edinburgh; educated as surgeon; served in East India Company. He settled in London as a general practitioner in partnership with Dr Neil Arnott. He graduated as D.M. in Aberdeen in 1815, and was admitted as Licentiate of Coll. of Phys. 1819. He settled in Russell Square and had a lucrative practice. He was an intimate friend of Sir James Mackintosh,[36] whose family gave Darling, for his assiduous medical attention to their father, a valuable diamond snuff-box which Sir James had received from the Queen

---

[36] Philosopher and historian (1765-1832).

Darling, George - cont'd. of Portugal. Darling saw Keats in Kentish Town (June 1820) and recommended wintering in Italy. Darling died at Russell Square 30th April 1862.

Clark, James Born at Cullen, Co. Banff 14th Dec. 1788. He went to school at Fordyce and then to the college at Aberdeen where he obtained a degree in arts. He changed from law to medicine and went to the Coll. of Surgeons in Edinburgh. He became an assistant surgeon in the navy, served in the 'Thistle', brought dispatches to New York and was wrecked off New Jersey. He returned to Edinburgh, receiving M.D. in 1817. In 1818 he accompanied a gentleman far advanced in consumption to the South of France. He became interested in the effects of climate on consumption. In 1819 he settled in Rome, became a well-known physician to the English colony. He saw Keats on arrival in Rome (1820) and was in constant attendance until Keats's death. He used a stethoscope (possibly in examining Keats) and referred patients to Laennec. Clark settled in London in 1826 and published a number of papers including one on Pulmonary Consumption, and in that year was admitted Licentiate of the College of Physicians. He became first physician to Queen Victoria in 1837, and an esteemed friend of Prince Albert.

He acquired the F.R.S. and was eventually knighted. The affair of Lady Flora Hastings - lady-in-waiting to the Queen gave Clark a great deal of anxiety. Lady Flora's abdomen became visibly swollen - assumed by court gossip to result from pregnancy. It has been suggested that Clark diagnosed pregnancy, whereas the

Clark, James - cont'd.

unfortunate Lady Flora died from an abdominal tumor. The *Lancet*[37] in a biographical note in 1870 suggests otherwise:

> If the secret history of the time is ever written, which is not to be desired, it will be known that Sir James Clark gave advice and counsel which if followed, would have dissipated the cloud which, for one moment only, rested on the honour of an English lady. But here, as in many other parts of his life, he sacrificed himself for others, and uncomplainingly bore a trial which he afterwards said almost killed him.

A further note from the *Lancet*[38] supports this view:

> all Sir James did was to suggest to the unfortunate lady that in order to silence the painful rumours then flying about, she should undergo a medical examination to discover the cause of these appearances.

Clark was often about the court;[39] the medical section of the University of London owes something to his work; so too does the science of medical statistics in his championing of William Farr who applied mathematics to sickness and eventually was appointed the first Registrar General.

Clark died on 29th June 1870.

---

[37] *Lancet* 1870. 9th July. p.67.
[38] *Lancet* 1870 16th July. p.67.
[39] *The Healing Touch* H. Williams. Cape. London. 1949. P.58.

Dr Luby   There is little information on Dr Luby who is mentioned only twice in Severn's letter to John Taylor after Keats's death,[40]

> On Sunday the Second day Dr Clark and Dr Luby with an Italian Surgeon - opened the body -,

also

> On the third day Monday 26th the funeral beasts came - many English requested to follow him - those who did so were Dr Clark & Dr Luby, Messrs Ewing - Westmacott - Henderson - Pointer - and the Revd Wolf who read the funeral service -

The London Medical Directory lists a Dr Luby for 1845. This may refer to Thomas Luby who graduated from Edinburgh in 1820. There is also a Timothy Luby from Tipperary included for 1835 and 1840 but there is no way of knowing if either of these could have been in Rome at the time of Keats's death.

There is one other contender who, purely on the evidence of time and availability is more likely to have been in Rome in 1821; but I have not been able to establish a direct connection between him and Keats. He is Dr John Luby, an Irishman, who obtained M.D. from Edinburgh in 1803. In 1806 he was assistant surgeon in the 9th Dragoons and in 1807 was superseded for absence without leave. He was readmitted in 1815 and became assistant surgeon 5th Dragoon Guards in 1816. He retired in 1816 and died at Windsor in 1824.[41]

---

[40] Letters ii Rollins. P.379.
[41] Index File Edinburgh M.Ds.

APPENDIX II

Biographies of Keats

Life, Letters and Literary Remains of John Keats Edited by Richard Monckton Milnes. 2 Vols. Moxon 1848.

John Keats A Study F.M. Owen. Kegan Paul 1880.

The Poetical Works and Other Writings of John Keats Edited by H.B. Forman. 4 Vols. Reeves and Turner 1882.

Life of John Keats William Michael Rossetti. Walter Scott 1887.

Keats Sidney Colvin. Macmillan 1887.

John Keats Albert Elmer Hancock. A Literary Biography. Houghton Mifflin. Boston 1908.

John Keats His Life and Poetry His Friends Critics and After-Fame Sidney Colvin. Macmillan 1917.

John Keats Amy Lowell. 2 Vols. Houghton Mifflin 1925.

The Life of John Keats Albert Erlande. Translated from the French. Jonathan Cape 1929.

Keats B. Ifor Evans (Great Lives series). Duckworth 1934.

Life of John Keats Charles Armitage Brown. OUP 1937.

Adonais: A Life of John Keats Dorothy Hewlett. Hurst and Blackett 1937.

Keats Betty Askwith. Collins 1941.

John Keats Edmund Blunden (Writers and their Work) No. 6. Longman Green for British Council 1950.

The Spirit of Place in Keats Guy Murchie. Newman Neame 1955.

A Doctor's Life of John Keats W.A. Wells. Vantage N.Y. Press 1959.

John Keats The Making of a Poet Aileen Ward 1963.

John Keats Walter Jackson Bate. OUP 1963.

John Keats His Life and Writings Douglas Bush. Weidenfeld and Nicolson 1966.

John Keats Robert Gittings. Heinemann 1968.

John Keats A Life Stephen Coote. Hodder and Stoughton 1995.

Publications with Particular Medical Relevance

An Aesculapian Poet - John Keats Sir Benjamin Ward Richardson. The Asclepiad. April 1884, p. 143.

John Keats Medical Student Louis Leipoldt. *The Westminster Review* April 1907, p.406.

John Keats Apothecary and Poet Sir George Newman. T.Booth Sheffield 1921.

Keats at Guy's Alfred G. Harris. Guy's Hospital Gazette 1925. May 9th, p.250.

Keats as a Medical Student B. Ifor Evans, T.L.S. May 31st 1934.

Keats as Doctor and Patient W. Hale-White. OUP 1938.

John Keats as a Student F.N. Doubleday. Guy's Hospital Gazette. 9th August 1952, p.312.

A notable case of Pulmonary Tuberculosis Anthony J. Daly. The Medical Press. Vol. CCXXXIII February 2nd 1955, p.98.

John Keats Trainee Assistant Special correspondent. *Medical World The Journal of General Practice* Vol. 82 No. 2, 1955.

Keats and the Hammonds Hamilton-Edwards, G. Letter to T.L.S. 28th March 1968.

Keats and Mercury C.T. Andrews. *Keats-Shelley Memorial Bulletin XX* 1969 p.37.

Keats - the Man, Medicine and Poetry Lord Evans. Brit. Med. Journal, Vol. 3, p.7-11, 1969.

Keats and Medicine Robert Gittings. Contemporary Review. p.138, 1971.

John Keats and Joseph Severn: The Tragedy of the Last Illness (Sydenham Lecture), Lord Brock. Keats-Shelley Memorial Association. (In pamphlet form) 1973.

Keats the Poet S. Sperry. Princeton 1973.

Evolution of the Stethoscope P.J. Bishop. *J.R. Soc. Med.* 1980. Vol. 73, 448-456.

Laennec: a Great student of tuberculosis P.J. Bishop. *Tubercle* 1981. Vol. 62, 129-134.

R.T.H. Laennec 1781-1826. His Life and Work: A bicentenary appreciation Alex Sakula. *Thorax* 1981. Vol. 36, 81-90.

In Search of Laennec Alex Sakula. *J.Roy. Coll. Phys. London* 1981 Vol. 15, 55-57.

The Poet-Physician. Keats and Medical Science Donald C. Goellnicht. University of Pittsburgh Press 1984.

Selected Bibliography

History of Edmonton Robinson. J. Nicholls & Sons, London 1819.

John Keats and the Hammonds. Gerald Hamilton-Edwards.
> (i) Keats-Shelley Memorial Bulletin (K-SMB) No. 17, p.31, 1966.
> (ii) K-S MB No. 12, p.21, 1961.

The Hammonds of Edmonton J.G.L. Burnby. Occasional Paper New Series No. 26. Edmonton Hundred Historical Society.

The London Apothecaries Cecil Wall. The Apothecaries Hall 1932.

Recollections of Keats by an old School-fellow Cowden Clarke. The Atlantic Monthly, Jan. 1861.

Memories of John Flint South Rev. Charles Lett Feltol. John Murray, London 1884.

The Colvins and their friends E.V. Lucas. Methuen & Co. Ltd. 1928.

The Evolution of Medical Education in the 19th century Charles Newman. OUP London 1957.

Keats & Embarrassment Christopher Ricks. OUP 1974.

History of Blood letting Fielding H. Garrison. New York Medical Journal, 1913. Vol. 97, p. 4327; 498-501.

Life and Letters of Joseph Severn William Sharp Sampson Low. Marston & Co. London 1892.

Letters of John Keats. A new selection edited by Robert Gittings. OUP 1970.

Haydon, Benjamin Robert. *Autobiography and Journals* Ed. Elwin, 1950.

MacGillivray, J.R. *Keats: A Bibliography and Reference Guide* Toronto University Press, 1949.

Rollins, H.E., ed. *The Keats Circle*: (K.C) Letters and Papers, 1816-1878. 2 Vols. 1948 - More Letters and Papers of the Keats Circle, 1955.

Murry, John Middleton *Keats*, 1955 - Studies in Keats, 1930.

Collected Essays No. 4 Robert Bridges. A Critical Introduction to Keats. OUP 1929.

Shelley Richard Holmes. Weidenfeld and Nicolson, 1974.

Keats's Publisher - Edmund Blunden. Jonathan Cape, 1936.

Index

Abbey, Richard 19, 31, 36, 41, 106
Aesculapius 59
AIDS 73, 76
Anatomy of Melancholy 87
Andrews, C.T. 24
Apothecaries 23, 25, 39, 42-44, 46
    Act 40, 44, 47
    Licentiate 50, 56
Arnold, Matthew 23, 113
Askwith, Betty 17
Auenbrugger 103

Babington, W. 67
Bailey, Benjamin 68, 77, 85, 88, 93
Bate, W.J. 18, 94
Birkenhead, Lady 25
Blunden, E. 17
Brawne, Mrs Frances 79, 96, 106
    Fanny 79, 80, 81-83, 89, 96, 100, 104-105, 106, 108
Bree, Dr Robert 100, 103, 117-118
Bridges, Robert 59-60
Brock, Lord 25-26, 74, 113
Brown, Charles Armitage 14, 55, 65, 67, 77, 78, 80, 97, 104, 111, 114
Browne, Sir Thomas 59
'Body Snatchers' 50
Bush, Prof. D.18

Cap and Bells 62
Chekhov 59
Clarke, Cowden 19, 32, 35, 37, 44, 45, 52

Clarke, John 31, 32
Clark, Sir James 26, 49, 101-102, 108-113, 119-120
Colvin, Sir Sidney 16, 19, 23, 24, 45, 113
Confessio Medici 39
Cooper, Astley 50, 52, 54-55, 63, 94
    George 50
Coote, Stephen 19
Cotterell, Miss 78
Cox, Jane 86-87
Crabbe, G. 59

Daly, A.J. 25
Darling, Dr George 105, 118-119
Dilke, Charles 31, 77, 97
Doyle, Conan 59

Edmonton 29-30
Endymion 17, 41, 61, 89
Erlande, Albert 17
Evans, Ifor 17,
    Lord 123
Eve of St. Agnes 62
Examiner, The 32

Frogley, Mary 86
Forman, Harry Buxton 15, 19, 20, 21, 93
Fothergill, John 46

Galen 99

Gee, Mrs Christina 11
Gittings, Robert 15, 19, 20, 24, 25, 42, 88, 93, 113
Gisborne, Mrs Maria 105
Goellnicht, D.C. 26-27, 63
Goethe 59
Gogarty, O. 59
Gonorrhoea 94
Goodall, E.W. 27, 62
Guy's Hospital 16, 40, 47-48

Hagelman, C. (fn) 26
Haemoptysis (bleeding from lungs) 74
Hale-White, Sir William 20, 23, 24, 25
Hammond, Thomas 16, 18, 19, 24, 34, 40, 41-43, 45-46, 56
  William 46
Harris, A.G. 23
Hastings, Lady Flora 108, 119-120
Haydon, Benjamin 67, 103
Hazlitt 85
Hewlitt, Dorothy 17, 21, 67, 90, 94
Hippocrates 98-99
Holmes, Edward 32
  Oliver Wendell 59
Hunt, Leigh 32, 52, 63, 104
Hyperion 23, 106

Isabella 61, 106

Jeffery, Sarah 64
Jennings, Alice and John 30, 33, 34, 36, 41
  Frances 30, 31
  Midgley John 31, 34, 76
Jones, Mrs Isabella 88-89, 115
'Junkets' 51

Keats, Frances (mother) 34, 35, 76, 85
  Frances (sister) 31, 65, 85, 97, 105
  George 31, 36, 45, 51, 67, 77, 78, 86
  Gorgiana 77, 85, 87
  House, Hampstead 96-97
  John
    appearance 51
    attitude to women 88-89
    birth 31
    biographies 14-27
    chooses Medicine 36
    death 114
    early sexual experience 91, 92
    epitaph 26, 113
    first haemoptysis 80
    physician v. surgeon 25, 52, 56
    rejects Medicine 65
    Thomas 30, 32-33
    Tom 31, 34, 51, 61, 76, 77, 98

Koch, Robert 49, 73, 75

Laennec, René 47, 100-101
Lambe, Dr William 105, 106, 118
Lamia 116
Lancet, The 56, 63, 120
Leipoldt, Lewis 21-22, 26
Lindon Louis 115
London Dissector 49
Lowell, Amy 16, 19, 24, 31 (fn), 94
Lucas, William 52
Luby, Dr 114, 121

Maria Crowther, The 78, 107
Mann, Phyllis 60
Maugham, Somerset 59

INDEX

Mercury 15, 80, 85, 93-94
Middlemarch 39
Monckton Milnes (Lord Houghton) 14, 115
Murchie, Guy 17
Murry, Middleton 69, 70

Napoleon 30
Newman, Sir George 23
Newmarch, Henry 51

Ode: to Autumn 106
  to Fanny 62
  on a Grecian Urn 106
  to Melancholy 91
  to a Nightingale 61, 63, 106
O'Donaghue, Abigail 97
Otho the Great 61
Owen, Frances M. 15, 21, 60

Pasteur, Louis 49
Piazza-di-Spagna (No. 26) 108-109
Ponders End 34
Physicians, Royal Coll. 40, 42

Rabelais, F. 59
Rawlings, W. 33
Religio Medici 59
'Resurrection men' 50
Reynolds, J.H. 65, 67, 86
Richardson, Sir B. Ward 15, 16, 20, 21, 22, 51, 93
Ricks, Christopher 37, 91
Rodd, Dr G.R. 97, 100, 117
Rome, voyage to 78
Rossetti, W.R. 15, 23, 94

St. Bartholomew's Hospl. 47

St. Thomas's Hospl. 47
Sainte-Beuve, C.A. 59
Sawrey, Dr S. 80, 95, 117
Severn, Joseph 20, 33, 51, 78, 106, 111-113, 114
Shelley, P.B. 13, 20, 93, 116
Siddons, Mrs 104
Smollett, Tobias 59
South, John Flint 49-50, 53, 55
Sperry, Stuart 26, 67
Stephens, Henry 20, 51
Stethoscope 49, 100-102
Surgeons, Royal Coll. 40, 42, 50
Swan & Hoop 30, 33
Sydenham, Thomas 99
Syphilis 24

Taylor, John 21, 66, 100, 106, 114-115
Teignmouth 60
Tuberculosis
  diagnosis 75, 103
  chemotherapy of 75-76
  immunity to 74
  pathology 73-74
Tyrrell, F. 50-51

United Hospitals (Guy's and St. Thomas's) 47-57

Venereal Disease 17, 24, 85, 92
Venesection 49, 98-100

Wakeley, Thomas 56
Ward, Aileen 18, 19, 26
Wells, W.A. 18
Wentworth Place 77, 78, 96, 97
Westminster Review 21